ASCADE COMPANIONS

he Christian theological tradition provides an embarrassment of riches: om Scripture to modern scholarship, we are blessed with a vast and omplex theological inheritance. And yet this feast of traditional riches is o frequently inaccessible to the general reader.

The Cascade Companions series addresses the challenge by publishing books that combine academic rigor with broad appeal and readability. They aim to introduce nonspecialist readers to that vital storehouse of authors, documents, themes, histories, arguments, and movements that comprise this heritage with brief yet compelling volumes.

RECENT TITLES IN THIS SERIES:

READIN
PHILIPPIAN

READING PHILIPPIANS

A Theological Introduction

NIJAY K. GUPTA

 CASCADE *Books* • Eugene, Oregon

READING PHILIPPIANS
A Theological Introduction

Cascade Companions

Cascade Books
An Imprint of Wipf and Stock Publishers
199 W. 8th Ave., Suite 3
Eugene, OR 97401

www.wipfandstock.com

PAPERBACK ISBN: 978-1-5326-7294-1
HARDCOVER ISBN: 978-1-5326-7295-8
EBOOK ISBN: 978-1-5326-7296-5

Cataloguing-in-Publication data:

Names: Gupta, Nijay K.

Title: Reading philippians : a theological introduction. / Nijay K. Gupta.

Description: Eugene, OR: Cascade Books, 2020 | Includes bibliographical references and index.

Identifiers: ISBN 978-1-5326-7294-1 (paperback) | ISBN 978-1-5326-7295-8 (hardcover) | ISBN 978-1-5326-7296-5 (ebook)

Subjects: LCSH: Bible. Philippians—Criticism, interpretation, etc. | Bible. Philippians—Commentaries. | Bible. Philippians—Meditations

Classification: BS2705.4 G87 2020 (print) | BS2705.4 (ebook)

CONTENTS

ACKNOWLEDGMENTS

I AM DEEPLY THANKFUL for the friendship and collegiality of Dr. Chris Spinks, my editor at Cascade. We have worked together for over ten years. Also, I wish to express my appreciation for Dr. Michael F. Bird, who has taught me a lot about Philippians through conversations, his scholarship, and some writing projects we are working on together. I wish to dedicate this book to Michael Bird who models the Philippian triad of Christian virtues: humility, unity, and joy.

1

INTRODUCTION

IMAGINE THAT YOU ARE the pastor of a church, and you invite an out-of-town friend (Mark) to preach at your church. He obliges and gives a very stirring message. Due to a busy schedule, he has to fly out immediately after the service. A few hours after he has left the church you get a text:

> Mark: *hey i had an awesome time with your church. Thanks for the invite*
>
> You: *it was great. We need to have u back sometime*
>
> Mark: *cool. Can you give your people a message from me?*

And then you see the famous DOT-DOT-DOT ("I am writing something" indicator).

And you wait for it. And you wait for it. And you wait for it . . .

It seems like an eternity has passed. And then it drops onto your phone. It is about four pages long. You are thinking several things at once:

> -*Why didn't he email this?*
> -*Does he expect me to read this from my phone?*
> -*Doesn't that seem kinda unprofessional?*

You look it over—it is additional thoughts on the topic that Mark preached. The content of the text message is actually pretty inspirational, but *why did he text it? What a weird way to send this kind of message . . .*

That scenario seems far-fetched. I can hardly bear to write three sentences on text. But this strange situation gives you a sense of what it was like for the apostle Paul to decide to convey his theological ideas *in letter form.* M. Eugene Boring reminds us that it was unprecedented for the early Christians to teach their values through letters. Boring wonders why letters became the dominant genre (e.g., letters in the New Testament attributed to Paul, John, Peter, and James, and in Revelation 1–2). He imagines that it could have been different. Why not a major focus on collections of Jesus sayings, or essays, or guidebooks of church order (like the Didache)? "In no other religious community have letters become sacred Scripture or played such a formative role."[1] Note how even after the first century, early Christian leaders continued the tradition of instructional *letters* (e.g., 1 Clement).

Why letters? Boring explains that "Paul and the early Christians adopted a this-worldly cultural form that functions on the horizontal plane of history."[2] This reminds us that Paul's letters, like Philippians, are not general abstract

1. See Boring, *Introduction,* 196.
2. Boring, *Introduction,* 197.

theological teachings. They are words of faith and life that came from a real person, in gritty, real-life circumstances (even sometimes from prison: Phil 1:1), written to real people (like Euodia and Syntyche: Phil 4:2–3) with real challenges.

When I am not reading and writing about the New Testament, I like to read the works of Dietrich Bonhoeffer. Bonhoeffer wrote many important books, such as the well-known *Discipleship*. But actually my favorite material by Bonhoeffer is called *Letters and Papers from Prison*.[3] Bonhoeffer spent the last several months of his life in prison, and during that time he exchanged numerous letters with his friend Eberhard Bethge. In several of these letters, Bonhoeffer reflects deeply on theology, the Bible, friendship, and politics. He also talks about various small personal matters, such as the conditions of his imprisonment, certain needs he had at the moment, and personal feelings. Bonhoeffer could not have imagined that his personal letters would be collected and published, let alone included in an official Bonhoeffer "canon." But students of Bonhoeffer, like myself, benefit immensely not just from reading his thoughts, but also seeing the way he processed life, raw and often spontaneously in the rough and tumble of life. And so it is with the apostle Paul and his letters. We might try to read Philippians or Romans to study Paul's "theology," but we would be foolish to neglect the fact that his thoughts come to us in the precious form of *personal letters* where we are permitted a window into the intimate connection he shared with so many churches and people through a mutual commitment to Jesus Christ and the "faith of the gospel" (Phil 1:27). So, with this in mind, what is the best way to read Paul's *letters*?

3. Bonhoeffer, *Letters and Papers*.

READ THE SITUATION

I am an amateur blogger.[4] When I have an idea to share, I write a blog. It serves as a kind of online repository of my thoughts on this or that. I think sometimes we imagine Paul's letters are like this—he had some general theological ideas he wanted to share and then wrote 1 Corinthians or Galatians. But, keeping in mind again that these are personal letters to specific churches or individuals, we must recognize that his letter messages are not generic like my "latest thoughts" blog posts. They are "words on target."[5] That is, Paul was something like a theological physician, stepping in to diagnose and treat churches with problems. Sometimes the problems were grave (i.e., Galatians; see Gal 5:4), sometimes the problems were less severe (1 Thessalonians). Nevertheless, they are considered situational—his letters respond to a particular situation. Therefore, those of us reading Paul's writings today need to pay attention to the background and context of his epistles.

Putting together the background and situation of an ancient letter can be difficult, but I find it an enjoyable challenge. Because we only have one portion or testimony regarding the situation (i.e., the Pauline letter), this exercise requires careful collection of relevant information and also some imaginative re-creation of events. I am a fan of detective stories. I like Sherlock Holmes, of course, but I also like a comedy show called *Psych*.[6] *Psych* is about a guy named Shawn Spencer who tries to help the police solve crimes by pretending to be a psychic that can catch criminals. While he is pretty good at the criminal catching, the show makes clear that Shawn is not actually a psychic. He

4. See www.cruxsolablog.com.

5. Beker, *Paul the Apostle*, 12.

6. USA Network, 2006–2014.

is just really good at using skills of observation to deduce who committed the crime and how it happened. When Shawn enters a crime scene, he takes in every little detail in the room, and then logically puts together the most likely scenario to create a theory of how the criminal did it. In a way, these are the same skills that we should use when approaching Paul's letters. We don't have all the information we might want, but there are many clues in his letters that help us to establish plausible theories about the *who, what, where, when, how, and why*.

When I study a letter of Paul and I want to figure out the context, I print out the text and try to identify as many contextual clues as possible. Here are some questions I ask.

- What do we know about Paul's history with this church? Did he plant/found the church?

- What do we know about the church to whom he wrote? What was their situation?

- Does Paul note any specific problems happening in the church?

- Are there any enemies or opponents (of Paul or the church) mentioned? If so, how are they characterized?

- Do Paul's warnings, advice, encouragement, or rebuke seem to relate to very specific issues in the church?

Sometimes some of the situational information is made explicit in the letter (1 Cor 5:1), but on many other occasions there might be helpful information that is more indirect. For instance, in Galatians there seems to be subtle evidence that Paul was coming under attack by rivals who put doubt in the minds of the Galatian believers. Paul opens his letter by describing himself in this way: "Paul an apostle—sent neither by human commission nor from human authorities, but through Jesus Christ and God the Father, who raised him from the dead" (Gal 1:1 NRSV). Here Paul does not come right out and say "My apostleship is being questioned, but I insist that I was commissioned directly by Jesus Christ." Nevertheless, the inference that his comment is reactive is pretty clear.

I encourage readers of Paul's letters to develop a situational analysis based largely on the most explicit evidence in the text, but I think some of the information can be tentatively filled out a bit more with subtle clues and indirect evidence. You might wonder—*why should I do all this situational analysis myself when there are many scholars who have already done this? Why reinvent the wheel?* Good question—after all, regarding Philippians, I will be presenting my own situational analysis in the next chapter! But I still suggest all readers of Paul practice this type of contextual study for two reasons. First and foremost, it puts readers in the mode of active attention to details. This is a good habit for reading all kinds of texts. Secondly, scholars disagree sometimes in their situation theories and—surprise!—scholars are only human. They make mistakes, they have biases, and they miss things. Developing your own situational analysis, and then comparing it to what someone else has come up with, is a healthy exercise for better study of Paul's letters in general.

READ THE RHETORIC

Rhetoric can be simply defined as "the art and practice of persuasion." It might be strange for you to think about Paul as a rhetorician, but in a way all humans are rhetoricians. We all try to use words to influence others towards a certain goal (whether it be raising money for a fundraiser, or convincing someone to go on a trip with you). Some of us may be better at it than others; Paul was clearly a master of words, and his letters developed rather sophisticated arguments. Think about it this way: in the ancient world, the average personal letter was about 100 to 200 words, basically one paragraph. Most of the information in a typical letter was mundane. *Hi, I hope you are doing well. How is this problem? Thank you for such and such. I need you to send me this. Farewell, and say hello to so-and-so.*

Now, for Paul, on average he writes about 2,500 words, and sometimes as many as 7,000.[7] That is a difference of about half a page (for a typical letter) compared to ten to twenty pages. So, Paul clearly had a lot to say. That doesn't mean he was long-winded as a matter of fact—Philemon is only 335 words. What this *does* mean is that, on many occasions, Paul needed a lot of words to develop the arguments that he wanted to present in order to get his readers to think and behave in certain ways in accordance with the truth of the gospel and the life of faith. Step one, then, is simply recognizing that Paul's letters had specific rhetorical aims. It is important to read a text like Philippians not as a general "devotional," but as a finely-calibrated set of arguments aiming to convince his readers of *something* in particular.

A second step would be to discern the flow of the text through its structure. Paul does not come right out and say: "Proof #1," "Proof #2," and so forth. So, again, it takes some elbow grease to break the letter down logically into stages of his argumentation. A quick word to the wise: while Bible chapter breaks can often be helpful guides, they are not perfect. (Paul did not put in the chapter breaks you see in modern Bibles!) If you want to work on a letter outline or flow from scratch, I suggest using a Bible without verse and chapter markers.

---

7. Richards, *First-Century Letter Writing*, 163.

A third step would be to look for tools in the rhetoricians' toolbox. Ask yourself, *what methods does Paul use to make his arguments?* Keep an eye out for such things as:

- Appeals to authority: such as proofs from the Old Testament or early Christian tradition
- Rhetorical questions
- Wordplay and word and thematic repetition
- Examples or models of righteousness or wickedness
- Hyperbole
- Metaphors
- Irony

This is just a sampling of Paul's rhetorical tools. Your mission is to pay attention to any and all means by which Paul attempts to prove his arguments about various aspects of the gospel and how it can transform the lives of believers.

READ AS A LISTENER

Here I want to make a rather simple point. We know that Paul expected his letters to be *read aloud* by the church that first received it (Col 4:16; Acts 15:21). Therefore, he not only wrote it in such a way as to make it pleasing to the eye (of the reader), but also so that it captures the attention of the hearer (or auditor). Therefore, even though most Westerners will read it *in English*, it is beneficial to sit and listen to the letter read aloud—or read it aloud yourself. Think about how listeners in a first-century house church would have reacted to various parts of the letter—*comfort? Joy? Frustration or offense?* When Paul sends "greetings," imagine what it would have felt like for your name to be read aloud in a letter unexpectedly. This exercise can be time-consuming, especially with some of Paul's longer letters, but I find it another helpful way to "experience" Paul.[8]

GET TO KNOW PAUL

It could go without saying that one of the best ways to strengthen your understanding of Paul's letters is simply to spend time getting to know *Paul*. Now, I know he is dead, so getting to know him in the flesh, as it were, is not an option. But we have several resources at our disposal. First of all, you have the collection of Paul's letters in the New Testament. You can learn a lot about his personality, his style of writing, his theology, his ministry, and his relationships by reading all of his letters. There is also the wealth of information in the book of Acts. While Acts offers the perspective of Luke, it still paints a picture of his passions, the shape and scope of his ministry, and many formative events that occured in his life. If you want one scholar's sketch of the life of Paul, check out N. T. Wright's *Paul: A Biography*.

LEARNING TO READING THEOLOGICALLY

In this guidebook to Paul's letter to the Philippians, we will give significant attention to the theological meaning of this text. Paul did not just want to give wise counsel for living a fulfilled life. He did not just want to solve social problems in a community. He did not just want to manage, curtail, or promote certain behaviors. His overaching goal was for his readers/auditors to faithfully, joyfully, and freely embrace the fullness of the gospel. And the fact that these situational letters became part of the Bible and passed on for many generations means that his theological messages have relevance

8. There are many good audio Bibles online (free). Here is one good option: https://www.biblica.com/bible/niv/philippians/1/.

for all believers in all places in all eras. Therefore, those who read Paul's letters from a perspective and purpose of faith are encouraged to read them *theologically* towards better knowledge of God and deeper communion with God.

Learning to read Paul theologically is not really about using a certain tool or method. More so it is about having a certain mindset in the act of reading, one oriented towards the work of God in the world. Michael Gorman has offered some questions for reflection when reading Paul in this way.

- *What does the text urge us to believe? (Faith)*

- *What does the text urge us to hope for? (Hope)*

- *What does the text urge us to do? (Love)*[9]

RESOURCES FOR STUDYING PAUL'S LETTERS

Below you will find some recommended resources on studying Paul in general. The majority of these recommendations are written by academics for laypeople.

Bird, M. F. *Introducing Paul: The Man, His Mission, and His Message.* Downers Grove, IL: InterVarsity, 2012. Bird is an excellent writer and offers a concise introduction to Paul and his theology.

Gorman, M. J. *Apostle of the Crucified Lord.* Grand Rapids: Eerdmans, 2016. Revised and expanded edition. In this lengthy introduction, Gorman offers an outstanding theological textbook that covers all major topics and issues in the study of Paul and his letters. This is more academic and more comprehensive than his *Reading Paul.*

Gorman, M. J. *Reading Paul.* Eugene, OR: Cascade, 2008. Gorman is America's leading Pauline theologian. This book is a basic treatment of Paul's key theological concepts.

Gray, P. *Opening Paul's Letters: A Reader's Guide to Genre and Interpretation.* Grand Rapids: Baker, 2012. Gray offers a basic introduction to reading Paul's letters *as letters.*

9. Gorman, *Elements of Biblical Exegesis,* 147–48.

Horrell, D. G. *Introduction to the Study of Paul.* London: T. & T. Clark, 2015. Horrell offers insight into how to study Paul in an academic manner and context.

Longenecker, B., and T. D. Still. *Thinking through Paul: A Survey of His Life, Letters, and Theology.* Grand Rapids: Zondervan, 2014. Much like Gorman's *Apostle of the Crucified Lord,* this is an academic textbook that comprehensively covers Paul and his letters.

RESOURCES ON PHILIPPIANS

These recommendations are mostly commentaries on Philippians written for non-academics.

Bockmuehl, M. N. A. *The Epistle to the Philippians.* Black's New Testament Commentary. Peabody, MA: Hendrickson, 1998. This intermediate commentary is a competent guide to the major interpretive issues and challenges in the study of Philippians.

Cohick, L. *Philippians.* Story of God Bible Commentary. Grand Rapids: Zondervan, 2013. Cohick has written a commentary full of exegetical wisdom, but also containing deep insight into how to "live the story" of faith inspired by this Pauline letter.

Fee, G. D. *Paul's Letter to the Philippians.* New International Commentary on the New Testament. Grand Rapids: Eerdmans, 1995. Many consider Fee's lengthy volume the most valuable exegetical commentary on Philippians, penetrating in expositional wisdom and burning with his characteristic zeal. This commentary is written primarily for pastors and scholars.

Hooker, M. D. "Philippians." *New Interpreter's Bible.* Nashville: Abingdon, 2000. This is a hidden gem, not widely known (due to being buried in a commentary that combines several Pauline epistles), but exceptionally well-written. At the end of each passage, Hooker (the writer on Philippians) includes theological reflections on the text.

Still, Todd D. *Philippians and Philemon.* Smyth & Helwys Bible Commentary. Macon, GA: Helwys, 2011. This series is visually stunning and offers a mixture of exposition and application. Still is a reliable scholar and winsome communicator.

VanHouten, Martha has produced an excellent, free online Bible study on Philippians that draws from the best academic scholarship, but is accessible and engaging for laypeople. See https://marthavanhouten.com/.

CONCLUSION

In this first chapter, before diving into Philippians, we took the preliminary step of thinking more widely about the act of "reading" and how best to approach Paul's letters. I hope it has clearly come across that readers (like you) are well-equipped to learn a lot from Paul's letters without immediately turning to modern "experts." It is helpful to sit down with a letter like Philippians and analyze it carefully on one's own. With patience and time, you will be surprised how much you can glean from Philippians through careful and close reading.

In the next chapter, I offer my own introduction to Philippians, breaking down the context and situation, purpose, letter structure, and key themes.

DISCUSSION QUESTIONS

1. Read through Philippians with attention to some of the features we have discussed above. Be on the lookout for clues regarding the situation. Notice and enjoy literary features like wordplay, repetition, and poetic elements. And start to ask theological questions like, "what does this text urge us to believe"?

2. What clues did you find that can help you piece together the situation?

3. What literary features did you notice?

4. What does the text urge you to believe? Hope? Do?

2

READING PHILIPPIANS
IN CONTEXT

INTRODUCTION

IN THIS CHAPTER, WE will set the backdrop for "reading Philippians." When you encounter a text, it is very helpful to understand something about the text, especially its author and its intended audience. And there may be contextual information that clues the reader into a more complete picture of the significance of the text. For example, one of my favorite stories is *The Lord of the Rings* trilogy. If you have read the books or even just watched the movies, you know it was first written by J. R. R. Tolkien. You may also know that Tolkien taught at Oxford University (UK). But did you know that Tolkien loved trees and despised the pollution and damages caused by industrialization?[1] That is

1. See   https://www.theguardian.com/books/2014/sep/19/how-

why the Ents (tree creatures) are heroes in the story and the Orcs carry out a destructive and toxic building enterprise. These kinds of details, I believe, help to enrich a story or text. When we look into the background of a biblical text, we can glean similar kinds of information when we learn more about the place, people, situations, culture, and text purposes. In this chapter, we will investigate such matters as they relate to Philippians.

THE CITY OF PHILIPPI

The ancient city of Krenides was renamed "Philippi" in 358 BCE when Philip II of Macedon (the father of Alexander the Great) took control of the city. About two centuries later, it came under Roman rule.

A Roman Colony

Near the end of the first century (30 BCE), Philippi became a Roman colony. With this rare, superior status came many advantages. Firstly, Roman Philippi benefited from Roman laws and enjoyed limited taxation from Rome. They received permission and funding for several public works such as a public library and local drama for entertainment.[2] Official citizens of the city were granted full Roman citizenship, but it is important to keep in mind not all residents were citizens to begin with. Many Greeks and Jews living in Philippi, for example, would not have been granted Roman citizenship.

---

the-west-midlands-black-country-inspired-tolkien-lord-of-the-rings.

2. See https://www.bibleodyssey.org/en/places/main-articles/philippi.

Roman Philippi was a popular place for retired veterans. Antony gave farmlands to Roman veterans in 42 BCE. Later, when Antony was defeated at Actium, Augustus renamed the colony after himself (Colonia Augusta Iulia Philippensis) and settled even more veterans in Philippi.[3] We can refer to the city of Philippi in the time of Paul as *Romanized*. While not all residents of Philippi fully benefited from it being a colony, it still bore a strong and pervasive Roman culture. This can be demonstrated in the discovery of numerous Latin inscriptions in and around Philippi (versus, e.g., Greek inscriptions).

A City "Full of Idols"

In the book of Acts, Luke describes Paul's horror when he entered Athens. He was "deeply distressed" because the city was "full of idols" (Acts 17:16). No doubt Paul would have had a similar reaction to Philippi. This city's strategic location on a major travel route (the Via Egnatia) would have brought influences of many cultures as many people groups visited and sometimes settled there. The traditional Greek and Roman gods were worshiped there such as Zeus, Athena, Artemis, and Dionysus. But there was also the Cybele cult (goddess of motherhood, fertility, and wild nature), worship of Silvanus (god of forests), and of some of the Egyptian deities such as Isis and Serapis. In Paul's time Philippi would have also dedicated a cult to honor the emperor. Scholars debate whether or not people actually worshiped the emperor as if he were a god, but at the very least the emperor cult involved temples and priests dedicated to ascribing "divine honors" to Caesar.[4]

---

3. See Bakirtzis and Koester, *Philippi*, 8.
4. See Winter, *Divine Honours for the Caesars*.

What this all means is that Philippi was a religiously diverse city. Like many of the major cities of the Greco-Roman world, deities could be found and worshiped for just about every type of desire or problem. Paul's proclamation of the gospel did not come to people unaquainted with religion; these were no modern "secularists." Those that turned to Jesus Christ must have found some compelling justification for forsaking their local and ancestral gods to (borrowing language from 1 Thess 1:9–10) turn from their idols towards one living and true God, and to wait for his Son to come from heaven, Jesus, the only one who can rescue from judgment and wrath (see Phil 3:20–21).

"Remember Me": A City of Status-Conscious People

Another feature we know about Roman Philippi is that the city cherished the Roman value of honor—perhaps to a fault. In the Greco-Roman world, honor was the most prized commodity. This involves social recognition and acknowledgment of one's social standing. Evidence for this value is literally all over the place in the remains of Philippi. We have discovered at least 700 inscriptions[5] from the area of Philippi.[6] Nearly all of these inscriptions were symbols

5. "Inscriptions" are defined as any writing set in one place and meant to be visible for public display. This would include items such as tomb inscriptions, honorific signs, and memorial altars.

6. Hellerman, "Humiliation of Christ": "Epigraphic testimonials to the social status of individuals abound in and around Philippi to a degree unparalleled elsewhere in the empire. Those who enjoyed positions of honor had an incessant desire to proclaim publicly their status in the form of inscriptions erected through the colony" (328); later Hellerman reasserts: "At Philippi, however, everyone who could scrape together the resources necessary to erect an inscription of some kind apparently felt the need to proclaim his achievements publicly . . . Residents of first-century Philippi felt strongly compelled to proclaim their social location publicly in the pecking order of

of public honor seeking to raise and display the status of a person, whether they were elite or a commoner. The following burial inscription, for example, was found near Philippi in honor of a freedman.

> Here lies Vitalis, first the slave, then the son of Gaius Lavius Faustus. I was born in his home as a slave. I lived sixteen years and I was a salesman in a shop. I was pleasant and well liked, but I was snatched away by the gods.[7]

All Romanized people experienced a single-minded, all-consuming zeal to acquire and demonstrate their status and honor, no matter the social level or occupation. Roman philosopher Dio Chrysostom (40–120 CE) states the underlying motive:

> For all men set great store by the outward tokens of high achievement, and not one man in a thousand is willing to agree that what he regards as a noble deed shall have been done for himself alone and that no other man shall have knowledge of it. (*Or.* 31.22).[8]

We must also imagine that this was the worldview and value system that the Philippian believers had when they heard the gospel from Paul. One can imagine, then, the shame, confusion, and perhaps even disillusionment when they suffered persecution from their family members, neighbors, and friends in Philippi (see Phil 1:29). In the following chapters, we will give special attention to how honor was reoriented towards Jesus Christ according to the Christian gospel.

---

this highly stratified Roman colony. Christians in the colony would hardly have been immune to these pressures" (336).

7. As cited in Dodd, *Problem with Paul*, 97.

8. As cited in Hellerman, *Embracing Shared Ministry*, 65.

THE "MAN OF MACEDONIA": ST. PAUL GOES TO EUROPE

Scholars tend to look to Luke's book of Acts in order to place Paul's relationship with the Philippians in the context of his ministry. According to Acts, Paul was busy doing ministry in Asia Minor (mainly modern-day Turkey) when all of a sudden he and his travel companions hit a spiritual brick wall (Acts 16:7). During the night Paul had a vision: a Macedonian man was begging him to travel over to what is now Europe and bring the gospel to save them (16:9–10). Without hesitation, they obeyed the vision, which almost immediately brought them to Philippi. The first thing Paul did was look for a community of Jews. While he did not find a synagogue, he did discover some women gathered to pray (16:13). A certain Lydia, a gentile who honored and worshiped Israel's God, was attracted to Paul's gospel message: "The Lord opened her heart to listen eagerly" (16:14 NRSV). She accepted the gospel of Jesus Christ and was baptized, she and her whole household.

This would have been an encouraging first encounter for Paul in a new territory, but not every one was this positive. On another day in Philippi Paul came by a slave girl possessed by a "spirit of divination"—her masters used her powers to make money through fortune-telling (16:16). This woman followed Paul and and Silas around for several days and harrassed them. Eventually Paul was fed up and cast the evil spirit out of her (16:18). Needless to say that the slave's masters were enraged at their loss of an income source and dragged Paul and Silas before the city's leaders. The magistrates had them beaten and put in jail—they even had their feet chained (16:24). But Paul and Silas did not lose heart. Rather, they prayed and sang hymns praising God. In fact, that same night a violent earthquake broke the foundations of the prison and even destroyed the prisoners' chains. Instead of immediately running for their lives, these evangelists ministered to one of the jailers, who believed and was baptized (16:27–34).

Eventually the city magistrates came to learn that Paul and Silas were both Roman citizens (who should have been treated more fairly and carefully).While they apologized to Paul and Silas, they also requested that they leave the city. First they encouraged their new Christians brothers and sisters, and then they departed (16:40).

Knowing this backstory can help us read Paul's letter to the Philippians. We know that there was conflict between Paul and the city leaders. When the slave-owners took Paul and Silas to the authorities, they accused them of political sedition: "These men are disturbing our city; they are Jews and are advocating customs that are not lawful for us as Romans to adopt or observe" (16:20–21). What would it mean, then, for new believers to "shine like stars" with gospel illumination in Roman Philippi (Phil 2:15)? How would their allegiance to Jesus cause disturbances in the city? We also know that God was at work, doing great miracles and changing hearts and lives, such as that of the jailer and the woman named Lydia. On that note, we turn now to talk about the Philippian church.

THE PHILIPPIAN CHURCH

It might be a bit misleading to refer to a "Philippian church." To some of us today, that might conjure up images of church bells, an organ (or worship band), a church building, pews and a "congregation." Instead, though, we should imagine a group of people (maybe 20–30 people total) gathered in a house. We only have a handful of names to attach to this believing community. From Acts we can only assume the presence of Lydia and the unnamed jailer. From Paul's letter itself we can add the names Epaphroditus,[9] Euodia, Syntyche, and probably Clement. In terms of social and economic class, most of the believers would have been what we think of as "working class," and some of them were probably slaves. Perhaps a few were men or women of elite status. In terms of leadership structure, it is peculiar that Paul mentions "overseers" and "deacons" in the prescript of his letter (1:1). The first term probably refers to those who had pastoral oversight of the community.[10] The second term, "deacons," probably refers to those who carried out caregiving ministry activities.

READING THE PHILIPPIAN SITUATION

We observed in the previous chapter that Paul did not set out to write general theological essays—in that sense he was not a "theologian." More accurately, as an apostle, pastor, and evangelist, he wrote letters to help believers to make sense of their life in Jesus Christ and persevere in faith, hope, and love embracing unity with their Christian brothers and sisters, rejecting false teaching and counterfeit gospels, and growing into righteousness, wisdom, and holiness.

If we try to reconstruct the situation in Philippi (again, see chapter 1 of this book for how we go about that task), we can make confident assertions about what was happening.

1. *The Philippians were facing local persecution.* In Phil 1:28–29, Paul refers to their suffering for the sake of the gospel, and the challenge posed by "enemies." We are not given details, but one can imagine that the Christians' ties to this new religion—and especially

9. Paul also names a "companion" (Phil 4:3); my guess, though, is that here Paul was referring to Epaphroditus.

10. See Hooker, "Philippians," 480.

their rejection of local and ancestral gods—did not go over well with family, friends, and neighbors. People may have refused to do business with them. Some may have run into trouble with the authorities, as Paul and Silas did (but perhaps without the benefits of claiming Roman citizenship). But a bigger problem would have been the *shame* associated with society rejecting them and treating them as pariahs. If they could no longer aspire to public honor, what hope did they have in life? (See above ["Remember Me"] regarding honor in Philippi).

2. *The Philippians worried about Epaphroditus.* He was sent from them to Paul to aid him in prison. They sent him with a gift (perhaps of food, medical supplies, and clothing). But we know that Epaphroditus ran into problems and almost died. They heard about this and feared for his life (see 2:19–30).

3. *The apostle was in prison.* Obviously the Philippians knew Paul was in prison. No doubt when he was in Philippi, they witnessed amazing works of God, and many experienced dramatic conversions (like Lydia and the jailer). But then their fearless leader (Paul) ended up in prison facing a potentially dire fate. This may have caused them to doubt, not only the future of his ministry, but also the joy of the gospel.

4. *There were troubles in the church.* We can surmise that there was some disunity or disharmony in the church. It was not at the level of a major split, but enough of an issue such that Paul had to call Euodia and Syntyche (two women leaders in the church) to come together in agreement and to set aside their differences (4:2–3).

5. *Were there false teachers?* There is some evidence that false teaching was a danger to this community. Paul

warns them about "evil workers" selling bad theology (Phil 3:2). It is unclear whether Paul was concerned about a present threat, a future one, or simply false teachers in general.

6. Given that most of the believers in Philippi were living at the subsistence level (e.g., hand to mouth), money troubles were probably common. But Paul mentions a delay in their gift-giving (4:10), which may have indicated a period of financial difficulty.

None of these problems on their own seemed to have been enough to throw the Philippian church into utter chaos. But it appears that the accumulation of all of these did take its toll. Before looking to how Paul's letter addressed these issues, it behooves us to take a closer look at Paul's imprisonment.

PAUL, PRISONER OF CHRIST JESUS

In his letter, Paul makes direct reference to being "in chains" (1:7, 13). Today we would say "behind bars," but Paul would have *actually* been in chains, likely chained to a prison guard. Paul does not mention *where* he was in prison. According to Christian tradition, he was in Rome, but others believe it makes more sense to assume he was in Ephesus. Paul mentions the "imperial guard" (1:13) and the "household of Caesar" (4:22), but these could refer to imperial associates in many major cities of the Roman empire.

We do know that Roman prison conditions were harsh. Diseases were rampant, treatment was cruel, and prisons did not supply food, medicine, or blankets to the incarcerated. That is why it was so crucial that the Philippians send their aid-gifts to Paul.

It is also instructive to know Roman imprisonment did not, in itself, serve as a punishment or sentence. No one was given a sentencing of "life in prison." Imprisonment served the purpose of confining a criminal until a trial and sentence—although the waiting period for trial could be lengthy. In Paul's case (he was imprisoned many times), he remained without absolute certainty regarding his fate (1:20; 2:23).

PAUL'S MESSAGES TO THE PHILIPPIANS

So what does this chained apostle argue in this letter to address their worries, obstacles, and challenges? Allow me to paraphrase Phil 1:27, which many scholars consider the primary command of the letter:

> Philippians, above all else keep this one focus clear in your minds: seek to live as a good citizen of Christ's kingdom with the gospel life and mission as your standard. You may be worried that I (Paul) will die, indeed you may wish for me to be there with you. My physical presence doesn't matter. What matters is that you learn how to stand firm in the faith bound together by the Holy Spirit, fighting the good fight side-by-side, pressing on to defend and spread the mission of the gospel.

Notice the clear and obvious use of political and military language. The image he supplies here is that of conquest. Not with weapons of the flesh, but the power of the gospel. When soldiers work together and believe they are winning, they push forward with confidence and courage. When they become intimidated, they hesitate and retreat. Paul calls these believers to trust that the gospel (as a new kingdom revolution) is sweeping the world and will continue to change the landscape of societies. Therefore, Philippians is a letter of hope and joy.

In the following four chapters of this book, we will walk through the four chapters of Philippians and examine more closely Paul's messages and arguments in his letter. Here is a basic rundown.

> The Gospel, despite our assumptions and fears, is unstoppable. It is like a rushing river unimpeded by persecutors, chains, and even the death of human leaders. (Phil 1:1–30)

> The story of Jesus Christ guides the way to what it means to live a victorious life that models humility, obedience to God the Father no matter what, and unconditional love for others. It is this kind of life that God honors and rewards. (Phil 2:1–30)

> The gospel demands, not a modification of values and allegiances, but a complete transformation towards cruciformity and Christoformity. True life and resurrection glorification only exist on the far side of conforming to the life—and especially the death—of Christ. (Phil 3:1–21)

> The God of the gospel is a God of peace. Many live with anxiety and fear, but Christians ought to be filled with joy, thanksgiving, and hope. Let us come together in partnerhip and worship to praise the God of good news. (Phil 4:1–23)

CONCLUSION

In the remaining chapters of this book, we will break down Paul's topics and arguments in his letter to the Philippians. In each chapter there are three sections.

Reading the Text. I provide my own translation of the text. The method I use is similar to that of the New Living Translation. I aim to communicate Paul's ideas in modern-day vernacular and style of expression. If you want to read a more formal or word-for-word English translation first, I recommend the New Revised Standard Version (NRSV), the New International Version (NIV), or the New English Translation (NET).

Studying the Text. Then I offer a running discussion of the text in its historical and literary context. In many ways, this is like a Bible study or commentary on the text. The focus remains on Paul's arguments, exhortations, encouragement, and advice in its ancient context.

Reflecting on the Text. Each chapter presents a substantial theological engagement with the key themes of the text of Philippians. The goal here is to discern how the theological messages of Philippians bridges the horizons of the first-century world of the early Christians as well as life today.

DISCUSSION QUESTIONS

1. Imagine you are Paul, sitting in prison facing an unknown fate. How would you feel about God? About your mission and ministry?

2. Imagine you are the Philippians, with your fearless leader in chains and you are being shunned by neighbors and rejected by family members because of your new religion. What parts of Paul's letter would be most comforting, reassuring, or inspiring?

3

CONFIDENCE IN THE UNSTOPPABLE GOD

Philippians 1:1–30

READING THE TEXT

Prescript: Greetings and Blessings (1:1–2)

> 1 Paul and Timothy, Christ Jesus' slaves—to all the holy people in Christ Jesus who live in Philippi, with special address to the communities' overseers and ministers. 2 May you be blessed by favor and peace from God our Father and from the Lord Jesus Christ.

The Blessing of Ministry Partnership (1:3–6)

> 3 I give thanks to my God whenever I think about and remember you 4 in every prayer I

pray for all of you, and it causes me to pray with celebration. 5 I experience such joy and thankfulness in prayer because I am blessed by your ministry partnership in the work of the gospel. You shared in my ministry from day one until now, 6 and I am confident of this: the One who produces this good work in you will see to a complete job at the end, the Day of Christ Jesus.

7 I know my thoughts about this are right, because you care for me so deeply in your heart, and all of you partake with me in a special calling by God's grace, sharing in my prison chains, and sharing with me the work of defending and proving the gospel. 8 God can serve as my witness that I care for all of you with the same deep affection Christ Jesus has for you.

A Special Prayer for Love and Wisdom (1:9–11)

9 And this is my special prayer for you: that your love will grow and overflow more and more with knowledge and deep insight, 10 so you can execute proper judgment regarding what matters most, and so be pure and innocent for the Day of Christ. 11 When you practice this superlative love, you will be filled up with the fruit of justice and integrity through Jesus Christ and you will glorify and praise God with your life.

Confidence in the Unstoppable Gospel (1:12–26)

12 Now, I want you to know, my dear brothers and sisters, that the seemingly unfortunate events that have befallen me have actually ended up advancing the gospel mission. 13 You see, Christ has become known because of my prison chains, put on display before the whole imperial

guard and everyone else here. 14 Furthermore, a great many dear brothers and sisters in the Lord have been given a boost of confidence to daringly preach the Message without fear or hesitation.

15 There are some who preach Christ because they envy me and want to make trouble; but there are also others who preach Christ with noble motives. 16 Yes, some preach inspired by love for me, knowing that I am here to defend the gospel. 17 But others preach Christ as rivals to me, harboring sinister motives, trying to stir up trouble for me while I am in prison chains.

18 So what? All that matters is that, whatever the motive, whether false or true, Christ is being preached, and that gives me cause to celebrate. And I look forward to more celebrations to come! 19 Because I know that this whole situation will end with God's deliverance, as you continue to pray for me and the Spirit of Jesus Christ continues to be supplied. 20 Indeed, I have every expectation and hope that I will not be put to shame by anything, but rather in my boldness, just as always before so also now, Christ will be honored and made great through my body. One way or another, Christ will be glorified, whether by my life or even by my death.

21 For me, living means living like Christ, and dying would be gain. 22 If I were to go on living in flesh, I would continue to produce fruit in my work, and I don't know which I prefer. 23 I am torn: on the one hand, I have a desire to leave and be with Christ, which would be a far better experience for me. 24 On the other hand, remaining in the flesh seems more necessary so I could minister to you. 25 In the end, I am actually convinced and know that I will remain and stand together with all of you to help you move forward in your faith and joy. 26 So then, when

I am with you again you will overflow in your pride in Christ Jesus.

Live as Courageous Gospel Citizens (1:27–30)

27 Keep your focus on this one thing: live as citizens worthy of the gospel of Christ; whether I come and see you in person, or simply hear about you from afar, I want to know that you are standing firm as one in the Spirit, with one united heart and soul fighting together for the faith of the gospel. 28 And I want to see that you are not intimidated in any way by your opponents. Your faith serves for them as a sign of their destruction, and for you of your deliverance—and all this is from God. 29 Indeed, it has been given to you as a privilege for the sake of Christ, not only to believe in him, but also to suffer on his behalf. 30 Thus you share with me in the same struggle, which you saw me engage with and hear that I fight now.

STUDYING THE TEXT

Prescript: Greetings and Blessings (1:1–2)

WHEN WE OPEN ANY of Paul's writings, we are immediately reminded that these are *letters*; they are personal correspondences from Paul to one of the churches (or one region of churches) in the Roman world. We tend to rush past Paul's initial words, assuming they are mere formalities, but Paul tends to preview key themes in his prescripts. For example, he refers here to himself and Timothy *not* as "apostles" (as he does in Galatians and 1 Corinthians), but simply as *slaves of Christ Jesus*. If we recall that Philippi was a highly status-conscious society, I think it would have been somewhat troubling for the first readers. Slaves were the least significant people in society. They were nearly treated as non-human. Some slaves *did* have special privileges and good treatment on occasion, especially if they happened to serve a good master and became a trustworthy confidant. But the vast majority of ancient slaves were "human resources," devoid of innate value except insofar as they carry out work and services. They had no respect or honor in society. This may have been Paul's way of deflecting becoming a symbolic hero for the Philippians. As a "slave of Christ," his life was oriented towards serving Christ and magnifying him (Phil 1:20). This was a lesson he wanted the Philippians to learn as well—later he portrays Christ also as a slave (Phil 2:7), serving humbly in obedience to God the Father.

Ironically, then, Paul seems to go out of his way to mention the leaders of the church ("overseers and ministers"). But we need to keep in mind that, (1) these were leadership functions, not offices, and (2) "minister" means "servant." Whoever fills these roles must remember that they are called to care for the church. In fact, the most "honorific" title is given to *all* the members of church—*holy people in Christ Jesus*. Holy status meant that a person or object had a unique and special relationship with God. They were transferred from the realm of the mundane and common ("profane") to the realm of the divine and sacred ("holy"). Angels were holy because they are heavenly beings. Priests were holy because they had access to the temple presence of God. Israel was holy because it was God's *special possession* (Exod 19:6). But with the gospel of Jesus Christ, with the presence of the Holy Spirit, *anyone "in Christ"* was now "holy." In biblical perspective, a "holy" status is the most respected one. The reality of this possession of holiness through the Spirit of Jesus Christ leads to another reality:

God cares deeply for his holy people, blessing them with grace and peace in Jesus Christ.

The Blessing of Ministry Partnership (1:3–6)

In the first main section of his letter to the Philippians, Paul encourages these believers by celebrating the commitment that they have had to supporting Paul's ministry. I cannot imagine that the Philippians were expecting such warm sentiments and jubilant feelings from someone who was sitting in a dank, cold prison with his hands in shackles. But the points he seems to return to again and again here is that *he is not alone.* They supported him every step of the way, certainly during his highest moments, but even here in his imprisonment. In a normal personal letter, one might expect Paul to talk about the conditions of his incarceration and his well-being—certainly they would have been curious. But he doesn't. In fact, he seems go out of his way to cheer *them* up—*God is hard at work and will see his work in you to the finish line.* And therefore *they* are not alone. Many scholars have pointed out that Philippians is Paul's most joy-filled letter. He aims to teach that Christian joy requires maintaining faith and hope in the God of the gospel even when present circumstances seem bleak.

Later in chapter 1 of Philippians we learn that they were going through a difficult period of local persecution (see 1:27–30). Here in 1:7 Paul encourages them by the reminder that, instead of being a curse, it is a privilege for them to share with Paul in the same gracious calling to represent the gospel. They share his chains by way of a ministry partnership (in prayer and giving) and they show solidarity in his suffering—later he says that they experience the exact same "struggle" or "contest" that he faces (1:30).

Philippians is full of moments where Paul "reframes" their perspective. From *one* angle, a situation can look one way (e.g., shameful, hopeless, isolating), but if you take *another* perspective, it can look quite different (e.g., glorifying, inspiring, unifying). It is also a beautiful thing to see Paul reach out to the Philippians in his role as a caring *pastor*. His heart goes out to them in their suffering and he reminds them that he loves them with a deep compassion that comes from Christ (1:8).

A Special Prayer for Love and Wisdom (1:9–11)

Again, demonstrating his pastoral vocation, the chained apostle lifts his hands to pray for the Philippians. He prays for love and knowledge. Looking at evidence throughout the letter, we get the impression that there were some problems with disunity in the church (e.g., see 4:2–3). While love was not altogether absent, neither was it abundant. For Paul what it would take to bring these Philippians together was proper discernment and wisdom. In the Roman world, a lack of unity often had to do with rivalry and contests of honor and power. This could happen at any level and in any context, so the church was not immune to these issues. Paul's prayer for love and insight is directed towards learning about what *really* matters in life—not petty squabbles or a game of "who is more important," but a life lived before God in obedience and humility. The evidence of a pure and true life is not the possession of power, but the fruit of "righteousness." The Greek word is *dikaiosynē*. While *dikaiosynē* is often translated as "righteousness," this English term has little meaning to modern people; it tends to carry a religious and archaic ring. Not so in the Greco-Roman world. Being filled with *dikaiosynē* would have been understood to mean either a public virtue of justice or a personal virtue of integrity—or (as I have translated it) both. Here again we see Paul reshaping their value system, as he orients their sense of virtue and value away from self-promotion towards glorifying and honoring God.

Confidence in the Unstoppable Gospel (1:12–26)

Paul devotes the largest section of chapter 1 of his letter to how he views his current situation. He addresses two potential sources of shame. First, he is locked up in prison facing an uncertain future. Secondly, there are some people around him who are stirring up trouble, trying to jeopardize Paul's life and ministry. Again, in a status-obsessed culture, either of these issues could be debilitating. Combine that with the challenges facing the believers in Philippi, and the Philippians might have wondered—*how is the gospel "good news" for us? Is this religion a blessing or a curse? Were we wrong to put our faith in the apostle Paul, seemingly a powerful leader, and now a lowly prisoner?* Perhaps they thought (echoing Gal 4:3) *have we suffered so much for nothing?*

Paul did not hesitate to respond with boldness and confidence: to the question of his incarceration, he flips their perspective. Not only has this situation *not* impeded his mission; it has actually propelled it. His imprisonment has brought Jesus Christ even to the imperial guard! Rather than discouraging believers near to him, it has inspired them to be bold! And what about troublemakers who harrass and undermine Paul? Paul does not despair, but rather celebrates because if they promote Christ, the gospel is still being proclaimed and that is all that matters.

When Paul refers to the expectation of his "deliverance" (which could also be translated "salvation"), he is not necessarily talking about a "happy ending" from a worldly standpoint. What he means is that he fully expects God to show up, but God often intervenes in unexpected ways. In any case, Paul claims "boldness," knowing that his one job is to honor and magnify Christ, even if that might be through death (Phil 1:20).

For Paul, he saw himself on the razor's edge between life and death, tipping easily one way or another by the winds of fate and fortune. As a thought experiment, he sets up a rough pro-and-con list. Dying would be "gain," since it would result in being with Christ. At the very least, his dignity would be restored. He would be crowned, not shackled. Rewarded, not rejected. Undoubtedly, Paul spent many cold nights in prison dreaming of that kind of freedom. But, as he turns to the "living" side of the list, he sees an ongoing ministry of living like Christ and embodying Christ's ministry in the world. Of course, Christ's life was full of suffering, but Christ's life was also "life-giving" to others. So, Paul recognizes that sometimes those hard choices have to be made for the better of the other—he must seek to press on in life to serve and stand with the Philippians.

Live as Courageous Gospel Citizens (1:27–30)

Most of the first chapter of Philippians is words of encouragement and blessing for the Philippians. In the last part of this chapter, though, Paul gives the primary exhortation of the letter: *live as citizens worthy of the gospel of Christ.* In the Roman world, Roman citizenship was a great privilege, and those who had this elite status were expected to hold to a high standard. So too with gospel citizens, Paul argues. Often translations will simply say "Live your lives . . ." But Paul chose a very specific verb that involves life lived as part of a specific social context—the city as a political unit (*politueomai*). Every Roman knew that good citizens care for the welfare of the whole society. Paul sets the standard for *Christians* as the *gospel of Christ*. The good news is, of course, all about the supreme Lordship of Christ, and at that time, being a good citizen meant loyalty to the sovereign lord. For Paul, gospel citizens seek to meet the standards of *their* lord—Jesus Christ.

Paul makes clear that good gospel citizens serve, stand, and fight *together* against any outside opponents that threaten their existence. In fact, they *cannot* defend their way of life unless they do so in lockstep and synchronized coordination.

Paul mentions his presence and absence because he was like their military general in the battle of faith—but in his incarceration the "troops" were losing their cohesion and breaking ranks. Paul encourages them to continue to work together to fight the good fight. They were facing public shame and rejection. But Paul boldly states that *their enemies* will perish and the Philippian *believers* will prevail, but they must trust the often invisible and hidden work of God.

The first chapter of Paul's letters begins the process of transforming the Philippians' imaginations. Many of them were trying to reconcile their Christian faith with their Roman values, and some such values were simply not compatible. The world would forsake an imprisoned leader, but Paul claims that God was using his chains to advance the gospel mission. The world would shun social deviants such as the Philippian Christians because they were honoring and worshiping a crucified Jewish criminal. But Paul professed that true life, joy, and peace could *only* be found in Christ Jesus. The good soldier and the good citizen care nothing except to serve the sovereign leader and promote the common good. Paul was reframing their perspective to focus on obedience to the one God, and dispelling fear of any enemy or foe who would inevitably be vanquished.

Reflecting on the Text

Thinking about Thinking

In the "reflecting" sections of this book, we will take a step back and consider some of the overaching ideas that are at work in Paul's letter to the Philippians. Christians have always believed that Scripture, while written *within* a particular time and culture, has messages that transcend that era and place.

There are a few Pauline letters where the apostle seems to write more overtly about a distinctively Christian epistemology and worldview (e.g., 1–2 Corinthians, Galatians), and Philippians is certainly one of them. Repeatedly Paul talks about knowing, thinking, and "regarding" truth and reality in a particular way (1:7, 9, 27; 2:2, 3, 5, 6; 3:7–8, 10, 15, 19; 4:2, 7, 12). Of course, it makes sense Paul needed to get back to basics, as it were, to help his readers see the world with new eyes. Over and over, with different churches, he had to deconstruct their false understandings of true worth, honor, and value; as he writes to the Corinthians: "the message about the cross is foolishness to those who are perishing, but to us who are being saved it is the power of God" (1 Cor 1:18). Paul uses an important Greek word several times in Philippians: *phroneō*—which refers to the direction or orientation of one's thought.

> "It is right for me to *think* (*phroneō*) this way about all of you . . ." (1:7)

> "Make my joy complete, be of the same *mind* (*phroneō*) . . ." (2:2)

> "Let the same *mind* (*phroneō*) be in you that was in Christ Jesus . . ." (2:5)

"Let those of us then who are mature be of the same *mind* (*phroneō*); and if you *think* (*phroneō*) differently about anything, this too God will reveal to you." (3:15)

"Their end is destruction, their god is their stomach, and their glory is in their shame. Their mind (*phroneō*) is set on earthly things." (3:19)

"I urge Euodia and Syntyche to be of the same mind (*phroneō*) in the Lord." (4:2).[1]

Why all this emphasis on "thinking"? It is as true today as it was two thousand years ago that we often absorb our perspective and value system from our cultural environment and we tend not to question it or judge it against another standard. It is like the proverbial fish in water—our worldview exists whether or not we are conscious of it. Indeed, it takes a fresh experience or teaching to jolt us into stepping back and *seeing* our cultural assumptions, for example when we travel to another country.

When it comes to the Philippians, we know they lived in a city and culture obsessed with status and honor (honor being a social value that requires recognition from others). There was a kind of cultural "ladder of success" to gain a higher status. One sought honor, praise, respect, and glory for oneself and one's own in-group (e.g., family, clan, community), but this was often at the expense of others. Honor was viewed as a "limited good," meaning that if *I* wanted to increase my honor, it was usually at the expense of someone else. For this reason, the vices of rivalry and jealousy were rampant. Everything became a competition for honor. We may give the simple example of the request of James and John to sit in the most honorable seats with Jesus (Mark 10:35–45). When the other disciples heard about this, they

1. All the cited translations here are NRSV.

became angry because there would only be two seats of honor (on Jesus's right and left) and James and John were trying to take them![2]

In such a context, success was guided by what we might call *anthrodoxia*, attracting glory for oneself from mortals.[3] Self-achievement, acquisition for myself, personal recognition: these would have marked high status. In that context, there would have been a constant sense of rooting for the other person to fail. Greek philosopher Plutarch observes that some refrain from praising a noteworthy speaker "as though commendation were money, [so] he feels that he is robbing himself of every bit that he bestows on another."[4] (We ought not to believe for a second that we "moderns" are more enlightened; just watch American political debates during election years where graciousness towards the other is absent and blistering attack prevalent.) Who can survive and thrive in an *anthrodoxia* world? And yet Paul himself was full of joy and celebration in spite of immense physical and social suffering, as well as rating rather low on the status scale from an *anthrodoxia* perspective. How can this be? One of the things that makes Philippians so theologically dynamic is the power of joy and peace that comes from God alone. Paul learned a secret, he says, of how to live with the right mindset (*phroneō*) in the world. And it is this he desires to pass on to the Philippian Christians. He wishes to give them the twin blessings of peace and joy. Peace is not just the absence of hostility or war; it is that feeling that troubles are not troubling and there is a

2. I was reminded of this example by Watson, *Honor Among Christians*, 79.

3. I have fabricated this word based on the Greek words *anthrōpos* (human) and *doxa* (glory). It refers to treating other humans as the judges of worth and seeking glory from them for one's self.

4. *On Listening* 44B (Seneca, *On Listening*, 236–7).

sense of calm and quietness in life (see Phil 4:7). Joy goes beyond that to the feeling that, not only is there peace, but also "things are going my way," life is showering blessings and good things on me (Phil 2:29).

Paul knew that peace could *not* be dependent either on one's life circumstances, or on achieving a certain status—both of these things are in flux and often out of one's control. When Paul calls the Philippians to live by the peace of God, it is a *forbearing peace*, peace that is not controlled by the maintenance of pleasant circumstances. This requires a worldview that is so stable and secure, it can handle the unexpected and unfortunate events that so often befall mortals.

Think of worldview like a grocery bag. Some are cheap paper or plastic, and if you get a heavy or jagged item, it rips apart and you lose everything (usually just a step before you get to the car). But the best ones are the reusable stretchy cloth bags. They can expand, and they can handle heavy or sharp contents. So it is with our perspective—can it *handle* or *bear* the troubles of life? The more *forbearing* our state of peace (which comes from God), the more capable we are of resisting distress and despair.

What Paul offers, then, in Philippians chapter 1 is what we might call a "peace" worldview. But how does one find this peace in a chaotic world? A world that can include prison chains? Paul gives five answers.

1. Build your life around a God-ward perspective

More than once Paul refers to living for the glory and praise of God (1:11; 2:11). He also points to the importance of the "Day of Christ," a future judgment day when human lives will be tested and weighed. Your neighbors don't define your worth and signficance. Your parents don't either, or your enemies or friends. For Paul, all of life is *unto God*—this is why he begins the letter, not by thanking the Philippians for their faith, but thanking *God* for his faithfulness (1:3).

Paul's own attitude is made crystal clear when he reflects on his uncertain future and the possibility of his demise. In his weakness and flesh, he might prefer to just die and end the shame and suffering. But, just as Christ himself said "not what *I* will, but what *you* will, O God" (Matt 26:42), so Paul wants nothing else but for Christ to be magnified, honored, and glorified through Paul, whether by his life or his death (Phil 1:20).

Today there are so many voices competing for influence in our lives, and so many platforms claiming to offer value. Some chase after the largest social media following, others on making the "right" kinds of friends or clients. In Galatians, Paul talks about certain Christians who promote circumcision and compel gentile Christians to be circumcised in order to be fully included in the faith. Paul criticizes the motives of these circumcisers. They are only interested in adding to their following and to "make a good showing in the flesh" (Gal 6:12). They are not interested in bringing them peace or joy, they only want to "boast about your flesh" (Gal 6:13).

Those who subscribe to an *anthrodoxia* perspective live and die by the rising and falling tides of popularity. They are like the proverbial pharisees who will only have the fleeting reward of their fifteen minutes of fame (see Matt 6:1–18), nothing lasting. But those who live only to glorify God—*theodoxia*[5]—are mysteriously free and content, even though the spotlight is never actually on them. They know that God's kingdom doesn't operate like worldly kingdoms.

---

5. This is another word I made up from *theos* (God) and *doxa* (glory); it refers to a value orientation centered only on what God thinks is important.

Again, to the Corinthians Paul explains that God chose to use—for the sake of his gospel—"what is low and despised in the world, things that are not, to reduce to nothing things that are" (1:28). Paul was not talking about metaphysics when he referred to "things that are" and "things that are not." He was talking about the so-called somebodies and nobodies of the world. Even Jesus himself fit the depiction of the prophesied servant of Israel who would have no majesty or beauty, despised and rejected, a "man of suffering . . . as one from whom others hide their faces he was despised, and we held him of no account" (Isa 53:2–3). But what made him powerful is self-giving by the will of God.

We live in a time and culture where we are seeing many entertainment celebrities, athletes, politicians, and even pastors succumb to vanity and greed. Their lives are wrapped up in accumulating personal glory at whatever the cost. We have often held these people up as our heroes and role models, but too many of them have ended up falling from grace. When Paul refers to certain bad role models in Philippians, he says that their "god" is their "belly" (3:19). By that he means they treat their lusts and desires as their ultimate authority. They think that accumulation of money, power, fame, people, and toys is freedom, but it is merely a reflection of their "belly" (or urges) controlling their life. Instead, Paul praises people like Epaphroditus and Timothy, who risked their lives to give to and serve others (see 2:19–30).

2. Trust in the unstoppable gospel

One of the most impressive figures from antiquity is Alexander the Great. In a very short time, he founded over 70 cities and his empire covered two million square miles. Did you know he died at the age of 32? One might wonder—*what else would he have accomplished if he lived to 40 or 50?* For as much as we might be impressed by Alexander's military power, he was, in the end, *stoppable*. If not by sword, then by health. He died of illness, perhaps typhoid fever. His empire was divided and fell into disarray soon after.

Imagine then also the apostle Paul, a charismatic, wonder-working, golden-tongued preacher of Jesus Christ, going from city to city, planting churches—gospel colonies in strategetic cities of the Roman empire. Imagine you are a Philippian resident who thought—*wow, there is something special about this guy.* You dive into this gospel message and tether yourself to Jesus and his people. *I could use some good news, peace, and joy.* And then . . . Paul winds up in prison, and things aren't going so well in Philippi either. This could be troubling and the Philippians very well may have wondered: *have we bet on the wrong horse?* But the strange thing is this: Paul is decisively at ease; in fact he sometimes *boasts* about his weaknesses, afflictions, and sufferings. He rattles off (what we think of as) setbacks as if they were awards: beatings, imprisonments, shipwrecks, bandits, persecution from false Christians (see 2 Cor 11:23–28). Why? Because Paul believed the gospel of Jesus Christ is an *unstoppable force*. So, in a way, Paul relishes when he faces an obstacle, because he *knows* God will find a way through it (even if the way is hard). So, *when I am weak, then I am strong* (see 2 Cor 12:10).

In Philippians, Paul uses his imprisonment as a parade example. While his incarceration could be seen as a setback, or worse, as an end to his ministry, Paul sees the opposite. He has been able to bring special attention to the gospel precisely *because* he is preaching and representing Christ, and he has been given "backstage access," as it were, to members of and workers within the imperial networks.

His shackles have not held him back, they have become conductors of the gospel's power!

Paul sees God's gospel like a mighty rushing river flowing down a mountain. Water is amazing. With its inherent dynamic ability to move and separate, combined with the power of gravity, nothing can stand in its way. It will find a way over, around, or through rocks big and small. The gospel flood is just like this, powered by the Holy Spirit and the hope of Jesus Christ. Nothing is going to stop it. In 1:12, Paul makes the Philippians aware that his chains have helped to *advance* the gospel. The word he uses here (*prokopē*) refers to forward movement, elevation, or progress. It is sometimes used of job promotions, where people aspire to "move up." Paul applies this thinking to the gospel mission—nothing can stop it from advancing. And if that is true, human servants of the gospel are *not* responsible for "converting" people or "forcing" the gospel through obstacles. So, what does Paul expect from the Philippian believers? *Keep up with that river!* Paul talks about wanting to help them progress or move foward (again, *prokopē*) in their faith and in their joy. Both faith and joy grow when God's people trust God to make good on his promises and when they dispel fears and doubts about the power of the gospel.

3. Whatever the circumstances, live boldly in mission

That leads us to the next theological theme we find in Philippians chapter 1. Paul emphasizes the relationship between Christian faith and *boldness*. Obstacles and challenges are not a reason to become cautious, hesitant, and shy. They ought to inspire courage. Paul came to observe that his imprisonment served as an inspiration for local Christians around him to preach the gospel with even *more* boldness.

They saw Paul's bleak situation, admired his resilience, and it gave them fresh energy to trust the unstoppable God and gospel (Phil 1:14). A handful of verses later he mentions that he too will dare to preach with boldness and confidence, even in prison, in order to make Christ known and magnified to all around him (1:20).

In view of this theme, we can see why Paul was attracted to using military metaphors in Philippians. In 1:27–30, he talks about "fighting" side-by-side and engaging in Paul's "struggle." This imagery was fitting, because in the Roman world, soldiers were held up in society as models of courage and determination. Roman soldiers in particular were legendary for their narrow focus on honoring the emperor and conquering their foe without hesitation or distraction. Paul was calling for precisely this kind of boldness. Whatever the situation, fair weather or tempestuous, good soldiers were guided by their orders and objectives. And they lived under the guidance and command of their superiors. So Paul was saying to the Philippians, *don't live reactively, quivering or questioning based on changing circumstances. Instead, carry out the work to which you were called with intrepid faith.* Later he more specifically identifies this work as holding tightly to the message of life (2:15), which probably involved living boldly according to the truth that God had revealed in Scripture and in the person of Jesus Christ.

4. Fight the good fight of faith together

Especially in the last section of chapter 1 (Phil 1:27–30), we see the military imagery most vividly, but it carries on throughout the letter (see 2:25). As we mentioned above, the idea of the "good soldier" was a common role model in the Roman world. One of the ways that soldiers achieved efficient and successful conquests is through their coordination and cooperation as a unit. Paul calls the Philippians to unity, probably with that image in mind: "standing firm as one in the Spirit, with one united heart and soul fighting together for the faith of the gospel" (1:27). Later, Paul writes something similar: "Fill my joy to the fullest by thinking with one mind, devoted to one singular passion, like two people sharing one body and soul, thinking as one person" (Phil 2:2). In almost all areas of life, we know that we are better able to accomplish our goals, and limit or overcome obstacles, if we work together. I am often reminded of a quote (popularly attributed to G. K. Chesterton): "We are all in the same boat in a stormy sea, and we owe each other a terrible loyalty." Put simply, *we need each other*. And Paul knew that. Sometimes we think of Paul as a lone ranger apostle, but the truth is that he was constantly surrounded by colleagues, friends, and ministry partners. They were not nuisances to him; on the contrary, he *needed* them. In Romans, he mentions certain believers that "shared his imprisonment" (Rom 16:7). Perhaps they happened to be incarcerated at the same time. Another theory, though, is that they *volunteered* to keep him company in prison. In any case, he talks about this as a serious relief to have their companionship.

Paul's second letter to Timothy is also written during one of his imprisonments. In that letter he recounts with a heavy heart that many of his confidants had deserted him (2 Tim 4:10–16). While Paul felt some encouragement by the presence of the Holy Spirit (4:17), still he called Timothy to pay him a visit as a trustworthy friend and coworker (4:13). *He needed people.*

Deep down we all know that "no man is an island," but when we are tired, angry, or stressed out, sometimes our gut instinct is to turn on one another. This was a danger for the Galatian church, for example, as they struggled with major theological questions that led to community turmoil. Paul warns them, "If . . . you bite and devour each other, be careful that you don't get eaten up by each other!" (Gal 5:15 CEB). Unity was not a brand-new, innovative idea with Christianity. Through this letter—and in many of his other correspondences, Paul appeals to a wider cultural value of unity and cooperation. For example, later he talks about a profitable relationship he established with the Philippians that involved "giving and receiving" (Phil 4:15). This refers to a mutually beneficial partnership, like when people carpool. Many Romans believed that what it means to be civilized is to live in a society where people help each other out and share public works and resources. What makes the church unique is the glue of the Holy Spirit and the guidance of the Lord Jesus Christ. In too many groups, organizations, and cities, leaders abuse power and set a bad example. But the Philippian Christ Hymn (Phil 2:5–11) demonstrates the humble example of Jesus who puts the needs of others before his own desires.

5. Look not after your status, but at your fruit

The final theological theme of Philippians chapter 1 involves what Paul presents as the *goal* of the Christian life. For many, then and now, "success" is quantified and calculated according to status, power, and stuff. But Paul argues that those are empty indicators of what *God* values. Final judgment will not take into account academic degrees (!), what is in the bank, or how many awards, trophies, or plaques have our name on them. In Paul's own words, he says "For all of us must appear before the judgment seat of Christ, so that each may receive recompense for what has been done in the body, whether good or evil" (2 Cor 5:10). Similarly, in Romans, Paul explains that judgment will examine human deeds: "to those who by patiently doing good seek for glory and honor and immortality, he will give eternal life; while for those who are self-seeking and who obey not the truth but wickedness, there will be wrath and fury" (Rom 2:6–10). *Wait a second. What happened to being "saved by grace"?* Of course Paul believed that works do not make someone right with God (Gal 2:16). Only Christ can rescue sinful mortals from divine wrath (1 Thess 1:9–10). But Paul treated final judgment as no light matter. While believers can stand secure that they will not face rejection or damnation from God, nevertheless, Christians will be held accountable to living out their faith in this world in service of God and the gospel.

In Philippians, Paul talks about this in terms of producing the "fruit of righteousness," or as I have translated it, "filled up with the fruit of justice and integrity" (1:11). Paul prays for the Philippians, not that they do good works, but rather that they walk in faith and love in such a way that the *Spirit* produces justice and integrity in their lives. The New Testament often appeals to horticultural and arboreal metaphors to illuminate the Christian life. The most famous of such is an image from John 15:1–8 where Jesus identifies himself as the "true vine" with the Father as the "vinegrower." True disciples are branches who must "abide" in the vine to be fruitful (15:4). The branches cannot do anything on their own; they depend on the vitality of the vine (15:5). But ultimately the branches do exist to produce healthy fruit (15:8). The "fruit" proves the healthiness of the branches (see Matt 7:16).

But what does this "righteousness" look like? Righteousness, at its most basic level, refers to *doing what is right*. It involves caring about justice in all areas of life. But on a personal level, "righteousness" often looks like what we call "integrity." This involves the conscious choosing of good, just, and generous behavior, even when no one is looking. Paul wants the Philippians to inspect the substance of their lives. It ought to consist of healthy relationships, acts of love and generosity, honest work and labor. He calls the opposite of this *kenodoxia*—empty honor or vainglory (Phil 2:3).

In the next chapter we will turn to Phil 2:1–30, where Paul gives more attention specifically to how Christ models humility, obedience to God, justice in the world, and personal integrity in all things. While Christ is considered by Paul a unique and divine person worthy of exaltation and the homage, he is also put forth as an example to emulate and follow.

DISCUSSION QUESTIONS

1. What would it look like for you to build your life around a God-ward perspective?

2. What would it mean for you to trust in the unstoppable gospel?

3. What evidence do you see in your own life that demonstrates that the Spirit is "filling [you] up with the fruit of justice and integrity" (Phil 1:11)?

4

ALL THAT IS GOOD GOES DOWN

Philippians 2:1–30

READING THE TEXT

Let Humility, Unity, and Love Guide You (2:1–4)

1 So then, if you have found any comfort from Christ, if any consolation from his love, if with the Spirit you have bonded, or to divine compassion and mercy you have responded—2 fill my joy to the fullest by thinking with one mind, devoted to one singular passion, like two people sharing one body and soul, and thinking as one person. 3 Reject any temptation to live according to point-scoring rivalry or self-glorification empty of substance; instead, let humilty guide you, each of you treating the other as if they

were your superior (and vice versa). 4 Each one should not be preoccupied only with their own concerns, but with the concerns of others.

Ode to Christ, Obedient Son, Humble Lord (2:5–11)

5 All of you should think this way, which demonstrates the example of the mindset of Christ Jesus.

6 Who once shined with the divine glory of God,

but did not cling to his divine status with a tight fist,

7 Instead he willingly made himself nothing

as when one looks upon a common slave, so he took the humble form of a mortal.

And just as he was found to be an ordinary human, 8 indeed he lowered himself,

becoming a subject to the point of death—even death by shameful crucifixion.

9 As a result of this obedience, God lifted him up on high,

and bestowed upon him a superlative title,

10 such that when all hear the name Jesus,

every knee will bend in the heavens, on earth, and below,

11 And every tongue will confess "Jesus Christ is Lord," And all this will bring ultimate glory to God the Father.

A Call to Obedience (2:12–18)

12 So then, my dear friends, even as you have already demonstrated obedience, especially when I was there with you, now it is even more important that you obey God in my absence. Just as I have lived out my hope of divine deliverance, so also you need to live out of your own divine deliverance, recognizing the presence and purpose

of God with holy reverence. 13 God is already at work among you, carrying out his will and his work as it pleases him.

14 In all that you do, refrain from grumbling and second-guessing. 15 You must show the utmost purity and integrity, like children of God who are faultless in the middle of a generation that is twisted and corrupt. In such a darkness you must shine like stars to illuminate the whole world. 16 So then, hold on tightly to the life-giving message—that way I can take pride in you when the Day of Christ arrives, because it means the apostolic race I have run, and all the labor I have done, have not been wasted. 17 But even if I must die, and my blood is poured out like a wine offering onto an altar, it will be spilled out upon the sacrifice and priestly service of your devotion to God; so I have reason to celebrate and happily toast your celebration; and, vice versa, be sure that you celebrate and toast me.

Sending Timothy and Epaphroditus: Paul's Trusted Coworkers and Models of Christ (2:19–30)

19 Now, my hope—Lord willing—is to send Timothy to you soon, so that I may be put at ease when he updates me on your situation. 20 To be honest, I have found no better ministry partner than he, as he genuinely cares about your situation. 21 Too many mortals care only about themselves, and ignore what matters to Jesus Christ. 22 But you know how reliable he is; he has devoted himself like a slave to the gospel mission, and has worked alongside me like a son with his father. 23 So, again, I hope to send him just as soon as I see how things unfold for me. 24

I am confident in the Lord that I too will come to you soon.

25 I think it is necessary to send back to you Epaphroditus, my Christian brother, coworker, and fellow soldier on the frontiers of the gospel mission; and he is your apostolic delegate and the person you sent to care for my needs. 26 The truth is, he was missing all of you and troubled, because he knew that you heard about his illness. Indeed he was very sick and nearly died. 27 But God was merciful to him, and God was also merciful to me, because if I lost him, I would been faced with such deep sorrow. 28 So I am all the more eager to send him back, so that when you see him again, you will be so happy and I will feel relieved. 29 Welcome him back, then, in the Lord with a big celebration fit for such an admirable person. 30 Remember that it was in his work for the sake of Christ that he came so close to dying; he risked his life to fulfill your church's commitment to care for my needs.

STUDYING THE TEXT

Introduction

THE MAJORITY OF THE first chapter of Paul's letter to the Philippians focuses on Paul's situation. Undoubtedly, the Philippian Christians were worried about him, and also worried about what the implications would be for the gospel mission. Paul addresses the uncertainty of his fate, but admits that he is full of thanksgiving, hope, and joy, because the gospel is spreading unabated, and it has been propelled by his chains. One can sense that even though the opening sections of this letter dwelt on Paul's imprisonment, what the apostle was *really* interested in was giving his readers confidence and hope in the unstoppable gospel.

The last section of chapter 1 (1:27–30) offers a hinge-point where Paul moves into direct instruction to the Philippians, challenging them, not to shrink back in intimidation and hesitation, but to move forward in hope and joy, working together as one community in the good fight of faith. This carries on into chapter 2. Eventually he calls them to fearless obedience to the gospel (2:12–18), but first he affirms the necessity of humility and unity, which comes to a climax in what scholars often refer to as the "Christ Hymn," but what I call the "Ode to Christ" (see below). Finally, Paul transitions to "business matters." He knows that the Philippians need help and encouragement, and he informs them he will send Timothy and Epaphroditus. It becomes clear, though, that this section is more than an addendum; the way he describes both these coworkers offers further examples of Christlike humility, self-sacrifice, and cooperation and obedience in view of the gospel mission. In a way, Paul may have also been trying to communicate that, even if he met his demise (2:17), they would have many different capable leaders to guide them.

Let Humility, Unity, and Love Guide You (2:1–4)

The first short section of chapter 2 begins in a kind of poetic or rhythmic fashion—which is why I tried to make it rhyme in English. The point seems to be that Paul wanted to bring them back to the very cornerstone of their being and identity—the love of God in Christ Jesus and the Spirit. They were given a great and gracious gift, but the gift expects the living out of a new life; or, to put it into the language of the first chapter, a new body politic. He expresses that his own joy would find its deepest fulfillment if he could witness their unity and cohesion, as if they acted together as members of one body (2:2). But what prevents a community from such cohesion and cooperation? One could easily guess the answer—selfishness, jealousy, pride, the unusual suspects. Specifically Paul mentions *eritheia*, which means "rivalry." Why would fellow Christians get caught up in rivalry? We have to remember that in the Roman world, everyone was constantly engaged in the act of seeking honor,[1] and this often came at the cost of competing with each other. (Again, think about the common practice of "mudslinging" in politics.) But Paul would have none of that. A "whatever-the-cost" pursuit of honor hurts the body of Christ, and therefore it hurts Christ. So also *kenodoxia*, what I translate as "self-glorification empty of substance." This empty glory is the hunt for status without any substance. Trophies without effort, grades without achievement, titles without experience. Empty glory might look good on the outside, but, just like an idol, is useless. *Instead*, Paul writes, Christians should be guided by *humility* (2:3b). Humility (*tapeinophrosynē*) does not involve "doormat" self-esteem. In a context where rank and reputation are *everything*, Paul turns it upside-down by telling them to treat *each other* as "superior" in status. This might seem unfair, but if *everyone* defers to the other, it subverts a stratified system where everyone pushes to be "first." In 2:4, Paul makes the issue clear: Christians should *never* say "not my problem" to someone else. Humans naturally protect their own interests, but the whole nature of the gospel defies this thinking—the self-giving God made it a priority to care for sinners, and we are called to carry out a ministry of care for others (as if they were our family members or our own selves).

1. See ch. 2 of this book, 14-16 (section titled "'Remember Me': A City of Status-Conscious People").

Ode to Christ, Obedient Son, Humble Lord (2:5–11)

Paul takes significant space to further dwell on what Christian humility looks like. What comes next is not just a description or example, but a poem or "ode" to Jesus Christ as obedient Son of God and humble Lord who became nothing to serve and redeem helpless mortals. This passage has been studied and debated extensively by scholars for hundreds of years. Some believe it predates Paul and was a part of "primitive Christianity," like an early hymn that Paul borrowed. Others think Paul used a preformed tradition, but modified and adapted it to fit into his theological points in this letter. And others still presume Paul himself wrote this text. While these conversations are interesting, all we know for sure is that Paul wrote these words as part of this letter. There is no reason to think that Paul *couldn't* have written this ode all by himself. Therefore, we will assume it is Paul's own message, though this doesn't discount the natural influences Christian tradition would have had on his thinking and expression.

Verse 5 sets up the reader's orientation to the ode: "All of you should think this way, which demonstrates the example of the mindset of Christ Jesus." The hymn is not *just* a worship song honoring the divine Christ, but *also* a model for Christians. Of course, no one can absolutely reproduce what Christ has done—his work was and is unique and divine. But Paul means that the best things in the world are worthy of emulation. Paul writes to the Corinthians, "Be imitators of me, as I am of Christ" (1 Cor 11:1). The Philippians were not meant to die on a cross or become divine. They *were* being called to shape their mindset and thoughts to model his humility and obedience to God.

The ode is designed like a cosmic parable. While for Paul the events are true (in that Christ really became incarnate, really died, and really rose again), he uses literary images and flourishes to paint that story in vibrant colors. In the opening scene (2:6), Paul conjures up the image of a glorious being in the heavenly realm. His divine glory shone like a star, reflecting his celestial status. When normal humans like you and me are imbued with this kind of power, our temptation is to cling tightly to it, like Gollum and the One Ring. Not so with Jesus. On the contrary, he willingly gave up that regal honor and radiant glory in obedience to the call of the Father to rescue the world.

In verse 7, the second act of this story, we are told Jesus emptied himself, or "made himself nothing." That *doesn't* mean he lost his "godness." In the context of this ode, it refers to extinguishing his radiant glory. Think of the famous story of the prince and the pauper, where an identical-looking pair (one a royal and the other a vagabond) exchange places. Once they swap, the prince is treated far below his original station. I am reminded here of when Jesus questioned the high priest after he was arrested, and one of the *guards* slapped him and said, "Is this the way you answer the high priest?" (John 18:22). Here, the king of glory (Jesus) is given a talking-to about etiquette towards the "high" priest. (The Gospel of John drips with ironic moments like this.)

The Philippian ode takes ample space to dwell on the humility of Jesus. The downward movement from divine glory to humble flesh was like a human king becoming a common slave (2:7b). What could be more degrading? Paul answers: death by shameful crucifixion (2:8). This form of Roman punishment was designed to be the most demeaning form of execution. In a world where honor was everything, crucifixion completely *wiped out* a person's reputation and that of their whole family. It was the scarlet letter times a thousand. Nobody *willingly* volunteers for the cross. But Jesus *did*, obeying the will of his Father to save sinners.

For most people the story would end there. But astonishingly the ode continues. God honors the self-sacrificing obedience of Jesus by raising him up, now to an even more superlative status (2:9). And he bestows a special "title" on Jesus: "Lord." Despite the humility of Jesus, lowering himself to the most humble station, in the end *all* beings will bow down before him. Christians obviously can never attain supreme authority like Jesus. What we *do* see here is that God honors those who obey him, who are willing to lay down their lives in love for others and obedience to him. As Paul writes, "All this will bring ultimate glory to God the Father" (2:11).

A Call to Obedience (2:12–18)

As the Ode to Christ focuses on emulation, it is natural that Paul urges the Philippians to have a mindset focused on obedience to God, just as Jesus was obedient—even to the extent of willingly surrendering his life on the cross. Paul is quick to encourage them that they have already shown faith and obedience in the past, but it seems that their zeal and confidence was somewhat dependent on the presence and leadership of Paul. Here Paul fills them with hope; even if he is gone for good, it is all the more urgent that they own their faith. Just because Paul is not in Philippi doesn't mean *God* has abandoned them (2:12b).

In 2:12 Paul says that they need to (in a more literal rendering of the Greek) "work out your own salvation." Does this mean they need to figure out how to *earn* their salvation? Of course not. The whole epistle is designed to give them encouragement, joy, and hope—stressing them out about earning salvation would be the last thing they need! We have to remember that the language of "deliverance/salvation" (*sōteria*) was already used by Paul in chapter 1 (1:19). Paul was trusting in God to take care of him, and he wanted them to walk in and live out their faith anticipating divine deliverance from their problems. Their suffering is not a sign of God's absence or silence. Rather, "God is already at work among you" and he is not ignorant of what his people are going through. He can use it to make them stronger (2:13).

In their suffering, Paul was calling them to grow up in their faith. So many people in the world live in darkness and walk around angry and cynical. The Philippian Christians are meant to shine like stars in this darkness, powered by the gospel message (2:15). In 2:17, Paul entertains the notion that he might die (2:17). But even in that unfortunate scenario, his death would not be a mark of shame or failure; rather, it would be given in honor of God and thus his spilt blood would become a liquid offering to God. And not he alone, but Paul also recognizes the obedience and self-giving faith of the Philippians which is like a sacrifice, pleasing to God. Far from being an embarrassment to lament, it is a thing to toast and celebrate.

Sending Timothy and Epaphroditus: Paul's Trusted Coworkers and Models of Christ (2:19–30)

Paul shifts back again to his own situation. On the surface, this can appear to be mundane correspondence details, which often appear at the end of his letters (i.e., tying up loose ends). Here it appears in a rather climactic point in the middle of the letter. First we will look at the details, and then we will examine more closely why he discusses these matters extensively at this juncture.

First Paul mentions his intent to send Timothy (who was already mentioned in 1:1). Paul was uncertain about his own situation (1:23), but expresses confidence that he will see them again (1:24). Then, Paul explains his intent to send Epaphroditus back to Philippi. They knew that he had almost died (1:28). He was homesick and they were worried, so Paul wanted him to go back home to support his Christian community. Paul may have been worried that they might feel he had returned prematurely (since Paul was still in prison with many needs). Thus, Paul seems to go out of his way to ensure they give Epaphroditus a hero's welcome rather than a slight or snub (1:29).

The final section of chapter 2 is more than just travel notes. In the letter to the Philippians, Paul populates the text with many models of righteous and unrighteous behavior. The "Ode to Christ" is the most extended example, but here we have these two men also lifted up as faithful disciples to imitate. Timothy is given several commendations. There is no better coworker, and his passion and care are unparalleled (2:20). There is not one selfish bone in his body (2:21–22a). He has devoted himself to the gospel mission like a slave, and has been faithful to Paul like a son (2:22b).

Next he commends Epaphroditus with several honorific labels. He is a Christian brother (as opposed to a false brother), he is a faithful coworker (as opposed to a worker of evil), and he is a "fellow soldier" who has risked his life for the gospel mission (2:25a). These are descriptions that pertain to how he relates to Paul. But he is also commended as a Philippian—he is an *apostolos*. This is a term that can be translated "apostle," but he was certainly not an official "apostle." It can also refer to someone sent out from a body as a ministry leader and their representative, hence I have translated it "apostolic delegate." All along in Philippians,

Paul was redefining their honor system. He was not saying that the pursuit of honor is bad (see Rom 13:7). The change comes with *in whose eyes* they seek to gain honor and respect—social scientists call this the "court of reputation." For most people, the "court of reputation" was the whole population, and especially those who stand in higher status than oneself. Paul shifts the "court" away from the *populus* and towards the one Holy God and the holy people of the church. Epaphroditus serves as a model of someone who sought praise and honor from God alone, coming close to death in obedience to God.

REFLECTING ON THE TEXT

Gloria in Profundis: The Moral Supremacy of Humility

In Roman perspective, there was no such virtue as "humility." Life's goal was to demonstrate superiority. The Greek word we translate as "humility" in the New Testament meant "lowliness" in the Roman mind, which smacked of weakness and inferiority. Think about it this way. In some educational systems around the world today, you have an assessment model where grades are limited. Let's say you have 20 students in a classroom. The teacher might say, "I can give 3 A's, 6 B's, 6 C's, 3 D's, and 2 F's." The students, then, *compete* for those 3 "A" slots. This is not a situation where everyone can get a perfect grade. It is a *competitive* environment. This might seem cruel, but it works that way in sports too: we rank players, teams get relegated in some leagues, and only one team wins the tournament even if severals teams do well. In the ancient world, everyone sought to prove their own superiority, especially in comparison to someone else. There was no "give everyone a trophy" attitude. Pliny the Younger, for example, demonstrates this when he writes "nothing is more unequal than equality itself" (*Epistles* 9.5). What he means by that is that it is actually *unfair* to treat everyone the same. Higher status people deserve preferential treatment, or else the fabric of society itself would collapse.

While much of the ideological foundations of America were based on a Roman political framework, the notion that "all men are created equal" is *not* very Roman. Life was like a big ladder leading to higher status and rank. One naturally had to climb over others (and even try to knock them off the ladder) to get to the top. What Paul proposes in Philippians, then, is rather remarkable. In 2:3 he tells them to stop looking up the ladder. Instead, *look down*. Even more than that, Paul advocates climbing *down* the ladder and pulling *other* people up. Christians, he argues, should be *preoccupied* with the glory and honor *of the other*, not oneself (Phil 2:4). Not long ago, my staff at work did a team-building exercise and the group leader said this: "Your job is to make the other people on your team look good." This is a remarkably counter-cultural ideology, which is why it has stuck in my mind. And Paul was proposing something similar. *What kind of world would we have if men commended women? If the older commended the younger? If race did not become a dividing line of status?*

For Paul the parade example is Jesus Christ (Phil 2:5–11). The humility of Jesus is portrayed as a downward movement from his glorious heavenly existence to the dust of the earth in the incarnation and his eventual death. It is crystal clear that the emphasis falls, not just on the condescension of Jesus, but his *willing* demotion. Paul uses a spatial paradox to talk about the upside-down kingdom. Most people do all they can to move up in the world. But here, in the Ode to Christ, we find a glorious, supreme being who proves his "highness" by going *down*. This is not the only place in the Bible we find this spatial paradox. It also appears with some regularity in the Gospel of John. The Fourth Evangelist repeatedly mentions that the Son of Man has a date with destiny when he will be "lifted up" (John 3:14; 8:28; 12:34). This *could* be interpreted as promotion, ascendency, exaltation. It conjures up imagery of supreme recognition, a great man put on display for all to honor and cheer. But the cruel reality is that Jesus's "lifting up" would be on a cross. He would be *physically* affixed to a wooden cross and raised up as a symbol of being rejected by Jews and gentiles alike. But if one reads John's story correctly, and picks up on his foreshadowing, this crucifixion is *in fact* his exaltation and coronation. The Romans would raise him up, but many will be drawn to this innocent man in fascination, admiration, awe, and worship (John 12:32). His crucifixion is not a mark of his shame, but a demonstration of his divine love.

I am not much of a poetry reader, but one of my favorite poems is entitled "Gloria in Profundis" by G. K. Chesterton.[2] This poem marvels at the work of God in Jesus Christ who conquered all by his humility and reckless love for lost humanity. Much like the Gospel of John and Philippians, Chesterton utilizes a spatial paradox. It is employed throughout, but appears even in the title. Many are familiar with the Latin expression, "Gloria in excelsis deo," which means "Glory to God in the highest." But Chesterton changes this to "Gloria in profundis." The word "profundis" means "depths." It can mean that we ought to glorify God *deeply*, as deeply as we can. But for Chesterton, it could refer to the opposite of the *highest*, hence one of his lines is "Glory to God in the Lowest." God is not low, but in the incarnation, suffering, and crucifixion he bottoms out, as it

---

2. This poem can be found online at https://www.chesterton.org/gloria-in-profundis/.

were. He does this willingly and unreservedly, and for this he deserves *highest* praise.

As a theological exercise, with one eye on the Ode to Christ (Phil 2:5–11), we will unpack each stanza of Chesterton's powerful poem.

> There has fallen on earth for a token
> A god too great for the sky.
> He has burst out of all things and broken
> The bounds of eternity:
> Into time and the terminal land
> He has strayed like a thief or a lover,
> For the wine of the world brims over,
> Its splendour is split on the sand.

Chesterton begins by talking about the greatness of God, too large even for the sky. He broke out of heaven to enter the "terminal land," breaking assumed rules about what it even means *to be the eternal God*. But like a lover he has *strayed* away from such conventions to be with the ones he loves.

> Who is proud when the heavens are humble,
> Who mounts if the mountains fall,
> If the fixed stars topple and tumble
> And a deluge of love drowns all-
> Who rears up his head for a crown,
> Who holds up his will for a warrant,
> Who strives with the starry torrent,
> When all that is good goes down?

Here Chesterton questions any mortal who seeks to inflate their pride, when God himself is humble. Who would try to ascend a mountain to be on top if the mountains bow down before the incarnate God? Who dares to search for a way to lengthen their height with a crown when "all that is good goes down"? This statement is nonsensical in a world where everyone strives for self-exaltation. But the gospel seeks to be the lens through which we see greatness.

> For in dread of such falling and failing
> The fallen angels fell
> Inverted in insolence, scaling
> The hanging mountain of hell:
> But unmeasured of plummet and rod
> Too deep for their sight to scan,
> Outrushing the fall of man
> Is the height of the fall of God.

This stanza sets up a contrast between the twisted (and inverted) angels who, in their attempts to attain ultimate power, fell, and the downward "fall" of God to rescue fallen humanity. I am almost moved to tears every time I read the lines: "Outrushing the fall of man/Is the height of the fall of God." How quickly sinners "fall" into sin, like willingly jumping out of an airplane without a parachute. I imagine Christ seeing someone dive out of a plane, and unbuckle his seatbelt and jump as well with speed and power to outpace the other's plunge.

> Glory to God in the Lowest
> The spout of the stars in spate-
> Where thunderbolt thinks to be slowest
> And the lightning fears to be late:
> As men dive for sunken gem
> Pursuing, we hunt and hound it,
> The fallen star has found it
> In the cavern of Bethlehem.

So finally Chesterton explicitly states: "Glory to God in the Lowest." All the power-hungry empires and warriors of the past had it wrong. True greatness is not actually found in demonstrations of dominating power. Rather, what mortals have been hunting for all along can be found in a humble cavern, a simple place, in the incarnation.

What does Christian Humility Actually Look Like?

We have to remember that Christian humility is not:

- *Doormat theology.* It is not low self-esteem, it is not "woe is me," it is not Eeyore for Christians. And it is certainly not putting up with abuse or harm.

- *False humility.* We actually don't do anyone any good when we have an outward appearance of humility, but arrogance lies within.

- *Low aspirations.* Humility is not the enemy of big dreams, challenging goals, and high hopes. All Christians should live by William Carey's famous words: "Expect great things from God; attempt great things for God."

So, then, what *is* humility? Recently I asked this question of my three children at the dinner table. It seems like a simple question, but we all struggled to define it precisely. It is one of those words where *you know it when you see it*. In one sense, it is simply best explained as the opposite of arrogance. An arrogant person thinks they are God's gift to the world. Yet we read in the Bible that "God opposes the proud, but gives grace to the humble" (Jas 4:6; 1 Pet 5:5; see Prov 11:2). What is it about the humble that God sees as salutary? It is not just a condition, like being poor or weak. Surely, it also includes some kind of moral or spiritual disposition. Looking at Scripture as a whole, I have found that the "humility" texts of Scripture seem to offer a cluster of traits of the humble.

The humble know they are not self-sufficient. The book of Revelation rebukes the church of Laodicea because they say "I am rich, I have prospered, and I need nothing" (Rev 3:17a). This is the attitude of the proud. God says to them, "you are wretched, pitiable, poor, blind, and naked" (3:17b). Until they learn that truth, they cannot know true blessing and wealth in God. We see this in the story of Israel, when Deuteronomy explains that God "humbled" his people by causing them to wander and acknowledge their reliance on him for manna "in order to make you understand that one does not live by bread alone, but by every word that comes from the mouth of the LORD" (Deut 8:3). Christians today practice fasting to serve the purpose of recalling that without God's help, God's people would perish.

The humble recognize that they are very small when compared to the greatness of God. David proclaims in Ps 8 the glory of the Lord and the mind-boggling magnitude and majesty of his works. He confesses, "what are humans that you are mindful of them, mortals that you care for them?" (8:4, my translation). David knows God has graced humans with such undeserving honor and privilege. The humble know they are unworthy, but they are grateful.

The best illustration of this is Jesus's parable of the Pharisee and the tax-collector (Luke 18:9–14). The Pharisee offers a self-inflating and self-congratulatory prayer to God. He dares to claim he is better than the person standing next to him. But the tax collector passionately confesses, "God, be merciful to me, a sinner!" (18:13). Jesus pronounces, "this [tax-collector] went down to his home justified rather than the other, for all who exalt themselves will be humbled, but all who humble themselves will be exalted" (18:14). One of the lessons here is that humility does not begin with a low sense of self, but an experience of the greatness of God.

The humble focus on care and concern for others. In Scripture, humility often goes hand-in-hand with gentleness towards and care for others. The proud, arrogant, and power-hungry expect and force others to serve them. The humble are always on the lookout to raise up the other. Jesus himself calls out: "Take my yoke upon you, and learn from me; for I am gentle and humble in heart, and you will find rest for your souls" (Matt 11:29). How can Jesus be humble when he is Lord? Humility is not about a *position*, it is a *disposition*, especially characterized by kindness and grace towards others. The humble, Paul writes, are clothed with compassion, kindness, meekness, and patience (Col 3:12; see Eph 4:2). The humble are too busy trying to better the lives of others that they don't have time to brag; they move around too much in search of aiding the needy that the spotlight can't find them.

Was Paul "humble"? Sometimes Paul has a reputation for being brash and even arrogant. But if we use the rubric above, the case can easily be made that Paul modeled humility.

Paul recognized his need for help, and his ultimate dependence on God. At the very least, as he wrote the letter to the Philippians while he was "in chains," he recognized that they cared for his basic needs of food, clothing, and supplies through their gifts sent through Epaphroditus (4:10–20). Regularly, he asks for prayer and appreciates the refreshment of Christian fellowship (Rom 15:32). He acknowledges that he is weak and his ultimate strength comes from God (2 Cor 12:9–11).

Paul confessed the greatness of God. In Romans he is clear that all are sinners, and yet God still died for "us"—he was no better than others (Rom 5:8). Paul held with him the weight of being "least of the apostles, unfit to be called an apostle, because I persecuted the church of God" (1 Cor 15:9). Paul knew the bondage-breaking, guilt-smashing forgiveness of God, but these memories reminded him that he was utterly undeserving of God's commission. God is great and gracious indeed.

Paul devoted his life to care for others. Paul makes clear in Galatians (1:13–14) that before he met Christ, he was on a fast lane to glory amongst his peers. God stopped him in his tracks and turned him around. He died to self (Gal 2:19–20), including death to self-glorification, "so that those who live might live no longer for themselves, but for him who died and was raised for them" (2 Cor 5:15). No statement in Paul's letters tells the story of his compassion for others more than when he states this about his fellow Jews: "I have great sorrow and unceasing anguish in my heart. For I could wish that I myself were accursed and cut off from Christ for the sake of my own people, my kindred according to the flesh" (Rom 9:2–3).

Conclusion

Philippians chapter 2 is largely about the virtue of humility, which supports Christian unity. Paul challenges the Philippians towards this (2:1–4) and then demonstrates humility in the mindset and life of Jesus (2:5–11). He challenges them to live in obedience without reservation (2:12–18), and then commends his coworkers Timothy and Epaphroditus, each of these serving as good models of unity, obedience, courageous faith, and humility, especially when it comes to putting others' needs and concerns above their own. There are so many cultural differences that separate Paul's world from our own, but these examples of humility are timeless. In every generation and culture, humans are tempted to focus only on their own concerns (Phil 2:21a). Narrow is the road for those who put others first by seeking what matters to Jesus Christ (2:21b).

DISCUSSION QUESTIONS

1. We discussed how humility is hard to define. But we tend to know it when we see it. Who is someone in your life that you would describe as "humble." Can you identify qualities, habits, or actions that lead you to identify them in that way?

2. Do you think the apostle Paul was humble? Why, or why not?

5

BECOMING FRIENDS OF THE CROSS

Philippians 3:1–21

READING THE TEXT

Beware of Taking Pride in the Flesh (3:1–6)

1 Furthermore, my dear brothers and sisters, celebrate in the Lord. It is no bother for me to write the same things to you, and it brings you assurance. 2 Beware, I say:

> Beware of the wild dogs!
> Beware of tricky evildoers!
> Beware of wound-makers!

3 In fact, we are the "circumcision" people, we worship tuned into the Spirit of God, and we look for honor in Christ Jesus and take no pride in our flesh. 4 Keep in mind, I could also claim

pride in my flesh. If there is anyone who might dare to take pride in the flesh, I would out rank them easily. 5 Take note of my resume: Circumcised on the 8th day? Check. A true member of Israel? Check. Moreover, I belong to the noble tribe of Benjamin, a Hebrew born of Hebrews. In my observe of the law, a Pharisee, 6 in proof of my zeal for Jewish piety, I hunted members of the church. As for righteous status according to the Jewish Law, I was faultless.

Christ, the New Standard of Value (3:7–14)

7 But whatever I had considered in my favor and for my honor beforehand, now all these things have lost their value when Christ entered the equation. 8 That is even putting it mildly. I have to treat all things that defined my life as worthless when I compare them to the vast wealth of knowing Christ Jesus as my Lord—by turning to him, I left behind everything, and to me they are worthless junk. It must be this way for Christ to become the new standard and summation of true value, 9 and now I bank on finding my honor and worth in him, forsaking any claim to a right standing according to the Law. Rather, it is through faith in Christ, a right standing bestowed directly from God received by our trust in Christ.

10 My aim is to know Christ, to experience his resurrection power, and share in his suffering, even imitating his kind of death, 11 and so mysteriously reach the final destination of the resurrection from the dead. 12 Don't misunderstand me. I have not obtained this or reached the final goal, but this is what I am pursuing in order

to catch it, because with even more passion did Christ Jesus grab ahold of me.

13 My dear brothers and sisters, I do not consider myself to have already reached this goal, but I have learned one key thing: forget what is behind me and continue to reach for what is ahead. 14 Focused singularly on the goal, I chase after the prize of obedience to the high calling by God which I pursue in Christ Jesus.

A Warning to the "Perfect" (3:15–16)

15 Whoever thinks they are "perfect," let us share such a mindset—and if any of you proposes another way to look at it, I trust God will reveal how you have thought wrongly. 16 But let us live in accordance with what we have obtained.

Choosing the Right Role Models (3:17–19)

17 Take me as your model to imitate, my dear brothers and sisters, and observe those who live with us as their life-pattern. 18 Be warned—just as we used to caution you on many occasions, and even now I lament having to bring them up again—many live their live as enemies of the cross of Christ. 19 Their fate is ruin; their "god" is their own belly, what they honor is actually their shame; their mindset is not spiritual, but worldly.

Hope in the World-Transforming Savior (3:20–21)

20 So you must remember that our commonwealth and citizen identity belongs to the heavens, and for now we long for and anticipate the coming of our rescuer, the Lord Jesus Christ. 21

He will convert our humble body into his glorious body form by the same power he will use to finally put all things in order in the world.

STUDYING THE TEXT

Beware of Taking Pride in the Flesh (3:1–6)

WHEN WE TURN FROM Philippians chapter 2 to chapter 3, the letter takes a rather dark turn. In chapter 2, we hear Paul's repeated encouragement to celebrate life, God, and one another, and to find hope in the many good and faithful examples all around including Jesus Christ, Epaphroditus, and Timothy. It is not long into chapter 3 that Paul transitions from celebration (3:1) to warnings of danger and evil that could lead the Philippians into trouble. The whole chapter is a meditation on Christian spirituality gone wrong, dependence on flesh rather than Christ, the pursuit of personal righteousness rather than faith in Christ, rejection of the cross rather than embrace of the cruciform life. These are not hypotheticals; in Paul's extensive ministry work, he had often witnessed such distortions and deviations from the "truth of the gospel" (as he puts it in Gal 2:5, 14).

Starting with Phil 3:2, Paul issues a threefold warning: beware of the wild dogs . . . tricky evildoers . . . wound-makers. This text raises many questions due to its terse expression. The first question is whether Paul is simply identifying false teaching in general, or if he is directly warning them about an imminent threat to the Philippian community. The reality is that it is probably both. Paul knows of itinerant false teachers who prey upon churches associated with him, but here in this letter this warning certainly identifies deluded religiosity and bad theology that could prevent them from experiencing the kind of joy that could uplift a chained apostle.

Who are these "wild dogs"?[1] Many scholars think that Paul was pointing to Jewish Christians who were attempting to force gentiles (non-Jews) to follow the Jewish Law and essentially "become Jewish" (in order to be fully acceptable to God). Why would Paul call them "wild dogs"? Jews considered dogs vicious, dirty, appetite-driven animals. Some Jews considered gentiles to be unclean "dogs" (see Mark 7:27–28). If the Jewish Christian false teachers were trying to convince gentiles to follow the Jewish Law, they may have told them: *you are no better than unclean dogs, unless you purify yourself with Torah*. Then, Paul would be "turning the tables" on them by referring to *them* as vicious "dogs," preying savagely on gentile believers. Simply by calling them "dogs," Paul was warning the Philippians to see sinister and savage motives that lay beneath a more proper and refined veneer.

Next, Paul refers to them as "tricky evildoers." Actually, a more literal Greek equivalent would just be "evildoers," but I added in the work "tricky" because Paul again is probably pointing out that they come under the guise of trying to help fellow believers, but in reality they doom them. They are not unlike Satan who masquerades as an angel of light (2 Cor 11:4).

Part of their evil work is identified in the third warning: "Beware of wound-makers." Paul's language here is a play on the word for circumcision. Circumcision is *peritomē*, and "wound-makers" (or mutilators) is *katatomē*. Almost certainly these men were trying to compel gentile men to be circumcised in order to find a right standing with

---

1. In Greek, Paul just says "dogs" (*kynē*), but I added the word "wild" to remind us that in the ancient world, dogs were not thought of as cute, cuddly, household pets and companions.

the God of Israel. But (Paul would say) if gentile acceptance is *only* based on faith in Christ, then obsessing over the cutting of flesh is no better than pagan rituals of wounding and scarring.[2]

Paul's warnings are important. On a quick glance, I bet such false teachers would be very attractive and convincing in form and word. Paul's words are for those with ears to hear and eyes to see. We have spent an uneven amount of time on 3:2 because this is the beginning of Paul's work in this chapter of provoking the Philippians to rethink how they see and interpret reality and what matters in life and before God.

As quickly as he describes these false teachers, so he briefly identifies the key features of proper Christian spirituality and religion. First, he refers to the Philippian Christians being the "circumcision" people—not that they all have been physically circumcised, but Paul is talking about circumcision of their hearts (Rom 2:29), and the special dedication to God that is marked by identification with the cross of Christ. In Colossians, Paul says that believers experience the removal of the "body of the flesh in the circumcision of Christ" (2:11), just as they were "buried with him in baptism" and raised by the power of God (2:12). Second, Paul says that they worship in the Spirit of God— God's people in Christ possess the Holy Spirit who bears witness to our human spirit that we are genuine children of God (Rom 8:15–16). Most importantly (for Paul's purposes in Philippians), true Christians take no pride in the flesh, but look only for pleasing and pointing to Christ (Phil 3:3).

2. I am reminded here of Elijah's contest against the prophets of the false god Baal. When Baal would not respond to the prayers and rituals of his prophets, they became desparate and "cut themselves with swords and lances until the blood gushed out over them" (1 Kgs 18:28).

More traditional English translations use the language of "boasting" here. But Paul's concern is not "bragging" in the modern sense. Rather, it is about identification with what brings honor and glory to oneself. Claiming pride in the flesh of circumcision or personal privileges is foolish in view of the world-transforming gospel. Paul shares a part of his own story of forsaking self-glorification through personal privileges. He rattles off all the ways he could have claimed pride in his identity: a pure and respected Israelite, of noble stock, with careful observance of the Jewish Law (Phil 3:5–6). Basically he explains here that right up until he met Christ face to face, there was no Jew who could claim more pride than he. In his own mind, he had checked all the right boxes of righteousness—the envy of his peers, the pride of his family, hero of his juniors. Little could he have known how Christ would completely shatter his world.

Christ, the New Standard of Value (3:7–14)

The previous section reflected on Paul's life "B.C." (Before knowing Christ), and with 3:7 we see his new life "A.D." (After Dying with Christ). Christ was not just a new friend or deity that Paul picked up to give his life added value. His whole world was turned upside-down, and all that he formerly valued went through an economic crash. Previously, his focus was on keeping the Jewish Law, respecting his ancestral traditions, and accomplishing those tasks that would put him in a position to "advance" in his Jewish culture in competition with his peers (Gal 1:14). But "A.D." his mind, heart, and will turned and focused like a laser beam on seeking to know Christ alone. His relationship with Christ became an all-consuming passion (3:8).

"Knowing Christ" was far more than simply acquisition of "knowledge," whether it be personal information, theological wisdom, or philosophical insight. What Paul here calls "knowing" (3:9–10), we must see as a deep and intimate connection and association. Paul saw in Christ a beautiful and unique power and he was drawn to this like a moth to a flame. But he came to know that the path to experiencing this power would be through sharing in Christ's suffering and death. Only then could he live in the "newness of life" with resurrection power (see Rom 6:4), and live in the hope of final resurrection of the body (Phil 3:10–11).

Though Paul had kept this lofty vision before him, he is quick to claim that he was still a work in progress, a pilgrim with miles to go. Some so-called "spiritual" people claimed perfection or elite transcendence. But Paul explains his perspective: *I have not reached the finish line, but I have learned not to look back* (3:12–14).

A Warning to the "Perfect" (3:15–16)

In the above section, Paul was clear that no Christian can claim to have arrived at final perfection. Until the Day of Christ, all believers are still on a journey to grow in faith, righteousness, and holiness (Phil 1:6, 10; 2:16; 1 Thess 5:23). So anyone who pretends to be spiritually faultless is fooling themselves. And yet, Paul happens to include himself here as one of the people in this group. Probably Paul was playing on two possible nuances of the word *teleios*. It can mean "perfect" (finished, complete, flawless), which Paul denies for present Christians; but it can also mean "mature" (experienced, wise, self-controlled; see 1 Cor 2:6). Certainly Paul considered himself mature, or else he would not be so quick to tell others to emulate him (Phil 3:17). Being mature is not first and foremost about *doing specific things*. Rather, it begins with and is guided by a particular mindset. When Paul refers to sharing "such a mindset" (Phil 3:15), he is pointing back to the transformation of values in view of knowing Christ (Phil 3:7–14), and perhaps even further back to the master mindset of Christ (2:5–11).

Those who try to use Christ as a platform for self-advancement or self-promotion are getting it all wrong. Paul urges believers to live in harmony with what they have received in Christ. He has already warned about certain false teachers who manipulate the Christian message to promote the flesh. Rather than glorifying Christ, it actually serves to undermine the gospel of Christ.

Choosing the Right Role Models (3:17–19)

As we have observed all along the way in Philippians, this is a letter of gospel examples, good and bad. Chapter 3 largely dwells on the negative, but here Paul calls the Philippians to copy him: "Take me as your model to imitate" (3:17a). And he is certainly talking about more than just idealizing his grand and glorious moments. He is referring to the whole shape, size, and scope of his "obedience of faith" (Rom 1:5), which includes his present sufferings in prison. And he also includes others who take the apostle as their life-pattern, people like Epaphroditus and Timothy (2:19–29), and others like Euodia and Syntyche who have "fought together [with Paul] in the gospel mission" as coworkers and whose names are written in the book of life as bold defenders and advocates of the faith (Phil 4:3).

But Paul also is quick to issue a warning. Here the horrible thought brings him to tears—some Christians live their lives in such a way they prove to be enemies of the cross of Christ. The reality is, if they claim to be Christians, they don't *know* they are enemies of Christ and his way. Rather, their distorted form of Christian faith frustrates the true work of the gospel. We don't know exactly *how* they reject the theology of the cross. But using 3:19 as indicators, it appears that they abhorred anything that might seem shameful (like Paul's imprisonment or Christian suffering) and focused only on how Christ could bring them glory and renown. They did not undergo the transformative value reorientation that Paul talks about in 3:7–14.

The way Paul describes these cross-enemies, they seek one thing, but end up ironically gaining the opposite. They claim to worship a "god" (a superior deity, God), but they turn God into an idol by refashioning religion in such a way as to serve *their* appetite for glory. They claim to have honor, but their disrespect for the true way of Christ is shameful. They believe they are spiritual and wise, but they are just another pagan religion under a different name and packaging.

Hope in the World-Transforming Savior (3:20–21)

In the last section of chapter 3 of Philippians, Paul brings his message back to his main thesis that these believers are meant to live as good citizens of the gospel kingdom of Christ (see 1:27–30). In 3:16, he reminded them that they ought to live according to the standards they had attained. In 3:20 he clarifies this by identifying their community as a heavenly "commonwealth." To claim a heavenly identity is not to live with your head in the clouds. No, it is more about knowing your *true* identity, even while you are a resident alien somewhere else. The Philippian Christians *live* in Roman Philippi, but their political identity is as full citizens of *Christ's kingdom*. To call it heavenly doesn't primarily refer to its ethereal nature. Rather, it means it is a greater place above and for now believers must live up to *heaven's* standards.

But God has not abandoned this displaced people. They live as aliens and strangers to some degree, but they live *in hope*. They expect, anticipate, and long for the arrival of the Lord Jesus Christ as a rescuer or savior. Here, I tried to avoid calling Jesus "savior," because in this context the word *sōtēr* has nothing here to do with a purely "spiritual salvation." Rather, when Paul mentions "commonwealth," and then "rescuer/savior," this triggers the idea of rescuing a captive or exiled people. It is about moving a lost or disenfranchised people back home, restoring their full sense of belonging. For Paul, Christian hope is not wishful thinking. Rather, it is longing for complete transformation and the restoration of *all* things in Jesus Christ (3:21).

REFLECTING ON THE TEXT

Did Paul Reject Jews and Judaism?

Philippians as a whole is a busy playground of theological debate. Scholars have invested much in dialoguing about the christological implications of the so-called "Christ Hymn" (2:5–11). When it comes to chapter 3, there is a long history of discussion about Paul's attitude towards Judaism, Jewish worship and rituals, and how he reflects on his heritage (3:2–6). Too many readers have hastily arrived at the conclusion that Paul was anti-Semitic (hostile towards Jews) or anti-Judaism (hostile towards the Jewish religion). Clearly, Paul was saying something negative about certain Jewish Christian false teachers (Phil 3:2), and he does reject *something* about his past in 3:7–14. But it is simply false to say Paul turned against Jews and Judaism.

When it comes to Paul's rejection of false teachers, we must remember that he often confronted, rejected, and corrected false teaching. False versions of Christianity tend to appeal to two vices: fear and pride. In Galatians and Colossians, the false teachings Paul addresses tried to convince Christians that they would not be safe from evil without Torah (the Jewish Law) as a hedge of protection. Fear-based "Christian" teaching tends to leave the center of faith (Christ himself) in order to protect the borders of faith by making sure every window is shut, and every door is locked. Believers become so worried about sin and evil getting into one's community and life, they take their focus off of Christ himself. So Paul repudiates fear-based false teaching.

Other types of false teachings appeal to pride. If fear pushes the person to the borders of faith (to protect it), pride puts oneself at the center, so much so that Christ is eclipsed. Faith becomes another context to draw attention to oneself. This is what we see in Phil 3:2–6. The false teachers about which Paul warns focus on pride and boasting, leveraging the Philippians' concern for personal honor and status.

This is why Paul repeatedly uses the word "flesh" (*sarx*). Flesh can refer to our skin and body. Paul did not believe the human body was evil or sinful all by itself. But because of sin in the world, "flesh" became a word associated with sinful appetites and cravings that tempt us. We can think of flesh as a centripedal force trying to draw all things to self—think of Eve, seeing how delicious the fruit was from the forbidden tree and knowing that this tree gave the power of knowledge and wisdom (Gen 3:6). Paul viewed flesh as the part of us that lives on an instinctual, often primal level. Paul talks about a war that happens within us between "flesh" and "spirit." He does not really think of these as entities separated into "body" (flesh) and "soul" (spirit). Flesh and spirit are like two voices inside of us. He presents them as forces battling within. "For what the flesh desires is opposed to the Spirit, and what the Spirit desires is opposed to the flesh; for these are opposed to each other, to prevent you from doing what you want" (Gal 5:17). But Christians know that they possess an all-powerful Holy Spirit that can conquer the flesh—but we must think and live by the Spirit (5:18), we must cooperate with the Spirit.

Coming back to Phil 3:2–6, what Paul criticizes in these Jewish Christian false teachers is their focus on the "flesh." Yes, they actually do promote circumcision as a means of obeying Torah. But Paul is more concerned about how all of this is *also* feeding the "flesh" voice within. Circumcision, when it becomes a mark of pride or honor, can easily turn into self-promoting pride. A badge of boasting.

Paul's Jewish Identity

In order to "show off" and demonstrate his ability to trump the credentials of the false teachers, Paul observes how he *could* boast about his pedigree and (former) commitment to Torah (3:5–6). He lists these items off like sections of a Jewish resume. The reader, we imagine, is meant to be impressed. It would be like me saying to academic colleagues, "I was born in Oxford, because both my parents were professors there; I went to Harvard as a genius teenager, and I got my PhD from Yale at age 25. Now I teach at Cambridge." When Paul talks about counting all things beforehand as loss or liability, that is not because Israel or Torah was evil. Rather, those things around which he based his identity and pride proved meaningless in view of what God has done in Christ.

To set the record straight, I need to say that Paul loved his fellow Jews, he treated the Old Testament as holy Scripture, and he respected the great examples of faith amongst his people. For instance, Paul used Abraham as the parade example of faith (Gal 3; Rom 4). Furthermore, in Rom 9 he expresses deep love for his people, and his desparate hope for their salvation (Rom 9:2–5). Later in Romans he mentions several fellow believers that are also Jewish, which he considers a special blessing to him (Rom 16:7, 11, 21). He expresses this more explicitly in Colossians: "Jesus, who is called Justus, also sends greetings. These are the only Jews among my coworkers for the kingdom of God, and they have proved a comfort to me" (Col 4:11).

What Paul rejects in Phil 3:5–6 is *not* his Jewishness, his love for Israel, or his heritage. The shape of his argument in chapter 3 is about pride, boasting, and self-evaluation. According to his former lens of self-evaluation, he was *faultless*. But he did not realize then that he was not truly living for God (Gal 2:19). He came to recognize that his life was bent on pursuing his *own* righteousness, and putting pride in his flesh by boasting in his marks of honor and his achievements. We ought not to blame "Judaism" or the Old Testament for this. The God of Israel clearly communicated to his people that true religion is about love for God, not rituals (Deut 6:5), it is about mercy, not sacrifice (Hos 6:6), it is about circumcision, dedication, and purification of the *heart*, not just the foreskin (Deut 10:16; Jer 4:4).

While Israel all along knew that they needed to bring more than dead animals and empty lip service to God, they still struggled with the problem of sin. Christ came to deal with this problem once and for all (Rom 3:25), but the atomic bomb of his death and resurrection not only obliterated the power of sin, it also destroyed any and all forms of in-group and achievement pride. So, we read in Paul:

> "for in Christ Jesus you are all children of God through faith. As many of you as were baptized into Christ have clothed yourselves with Christ. There is no longer Jew or Greek, there is no longer slave or free, there is no longer male and

female; for all of you are one in Christ Jesus."
(Gal 3:26–28)

"So if anyone is in Christ, there is a new creation:
everything old has passed away; see, everything
has become new!" (2 Cor 5:17)

From this we can see Paul's "loss" of all things (Phil 3:7–8)
is not really about Judaism or Jewishness after all; the
cosmos-transforming impact of life in Christ has rendered
every -ism or -ness null.

Christ, the Costly Pearl:
The Price of Becoming Friends of the Cross

Paul's life transformation is more than choosing a new
hobby, adding a new value, or changing behaviors. It is
an epistemological revolution. Twenty years ago, I would
insert an analogy from the 1999 movie *The Matrix*, but I
can think of a better and more recent example—the 2016
Marvel movie *Doctor Strange*. Dr. Strange was a brilliant,
if cocky, brain surgeon who lived according to science and
scoffed at religion and spirituality. Everything, he thought,
could be explained or fixed by science. After a horrible car
accident rendered his surgical hands useless, he spent his
fortune on finding a medical solution—to no avail. With
his last few pennies and just a shred of hope, he travels to
Tibet in pursuit of a rumored healer who could repair such
hopeless injuries. When he finds the Ancient One, at first
he thinks she is crazy, because she claims his answers can
be found in mysticism and sorcery. She finally *shows* him
real sorcery and magic and Strange becomes a believer,
eventually counteracting his debilitating injuries through
mystical powers. There is nothing particularly *Christian*
about this movie, but what I find resonant with Paul's story

is the complete reversal of perspective. Everything Strange *used* to believe led him to treat the Ancient One as a crazy person. Once his eyes were opened, he had to dismantle the entire structure of what he knew was true and false.

That example, while entertaining, might seem too fanciful to help us think through a complete change of value and worth, so consider this. In the Pacific Northwest, we regularly see news that warns of an impending Cascadia earthquake that is due to rock our world. It might happen in forty years, it might happen tomorrow. My family went to a Red Cross information meeting to learn how to prepare for this event. One of the clear messages was this: *it is not going to be just inconvenient or disruptive, it will change everything*. If this quake hits with the force seismologists predict, buildings will collapse, roads will disappear, powerlines and cell towers will go down. Portland (where I live) will be pulled back into the dark ages. All the resources and systems of value we hold dear will be obsolete for a good while. That means: no credit cards, no banks, no ATMS, probably no cars, no internet, no phone. For that time, a $10 crowbar would be more valuable than my fancy smartphone. Imagine, in the midst of the wreckage, you look at all the supposedly valuable things you have worked so hard to buy and collect (especially gadgets), and now they are depleted of their worth in a terrible minute.

Surely this is similar to what happened to Paul—but there was no Red Cross emergency preparedness seminar. The Christ-quake just happened and he was left to figure out what matters in this new reality. But Paul laments that many believers still tried to carry on protecting their valuables. We might think of this problem as a kind of cultural syncretism, mixing Jesus into our cultural values, ideologies, and gods to create a brand-new (warped) religion. So, we see even today the "Jesus" who promotes democracy.

The "Jesus" who hates Jews. The "Jesus" who loves guns. The name of Jesus is used as a tool to legitimize many worldly values or ideologies. In such cases, the value system is not comprehensively audited; rather, Jesus is dumped onto it.

We get the sense that this was going on in Corinth, for example. Believers were rallying around certain leaders (Paul, Apollos, Cephas), and competing for the best "team" (1 Cor 1:10). The meal of the Lord's Supper also became a context for showing off elitism and superiority. Paul refers to some believers stuffing themselves with food, and getting drunk on wine, while others starve, the kind of antics that regularly happened at Roman dinner parties where the upper crust got the best treatment and those lower on the echelon fought for scraps (see 1 Cor 11:21–22). Notice how David Garland diagnoses the problems that some of the Corinthians had.

> It is likely that they flaunted their symbols of status, wisdom, influence, and family pedigree and looked down on others of lesser status. They appear to have wanted to preserve the social barriers of class and status that permeated their social world . . . For some, the Christian community had become simply another arena to compete for status according to the societal norms.[3]

This is the kind of cultural syncretism, the "mixing" of Jesus into dominant societal values, that we described earlier. Paul's approach to jolting the Corinthians into rethinking their whole value system was to build the gospel message around the cross. Martin Luther had a famous saying: *crux sola est nostra theologia*: "the cross alone is our theology." By that he meant that the crucifixion of Jesus teaches us the core understanding of the essence of Christian faith. Luther

---

3. Garland, *1 Corinthians*, 6.

called for true theologians to be theologians of the cross. As opposed to what? Theologians of *glory*. Theologians of glory seek to conform Christianity to worldly forms of power, glory, and pride. Theologians of the cross understand the subversive nature of faith. In the cross, God shatters and displaces worldly ways of establishing honor and value. The cross, from a worldly perspective, is utter nonsense (1 Cor 1:18). When Paul had to reckon with the crucified God, he knew that the ideological construct he once had could not have been correct. So, instead of rejecting the cross, he embraced it. But little did he know he would be dogged by Christian false teachers whom he calls *enemies of the cross.* They are Luther's *theologians of glory.* That is, they paste Christ onto a worldly value system. So they feed their appetites for fame and power.

If true Christians are not enemies of the cross, what ought they to be? Friends of the cross. Friends of the cross are disciples who take up their crosses and follow Jesus. They do not hide the cross or dismiss it. They know that people who want to truly know Christ must become like Christ in his sufferings and become like him in his death. But what does *that* mean? It does not mean pain for the sake of pain—if God is Father, he hates to see his children suffer. But if Christians are going to conform to the healthy image of the Son (Rom 8:29), then they need to endure a painful formation process. That requires imitating and trying to emulate Jesus in a sinful world, and that requires suffering, because students (Christians) are no better than their teacher (Jesus). If Jesus was persecuted and rejected, so too will his followers be rejected.

In Galatians, Paul refers rather extensively to what it means to be "friends of the cross." Such disciples have "crucified the flesh with its passions and desires" (Gal 5:24). They confront the desires of the flesh and put them to death. This is literally an excruciating process, because it requires exposing oneself to vulnerability and weakness. Paul talks to the Galatians about his being crucified with Christ and dying to self so Christ can take up residence and life in him (Gal 2:19–20). Later he confesses: "May I never boast of anything except the cross of our Lord Jesus Christ, by which the world has been crucified to me, and I to the world" (Gal 6:14). This tender statement from Paul resonates closely with what he tells the Philippians. Gaining and knowing Christ is the greatest treasure in the world, but it comes at a cost—crucifixion and death to self. Death to self does not mean "I" am not important. It means I cannot collect and take pride in *my own* glory.

When I think about the central message of Philippians chapter 3, I think of Matthew's parable of the pearl of great price, or the costly pearl. This two-verse story is about a merchant in search for rare and valuable pearls. When he came across a costly pearl, he sold *all that he had* and bought it (Matt 13:45–46). The reader is left to wonder how this merchant survived without his money or his possessions. *What kind of treasure would lead him to make such a foolish choice?* Paul treats *Christ* as that kind of costly pearl, of such beauty and worth that nothing in the whole world can compare. But acquiring it comes at a hefty price—one must forsake and divest of *all other valuables* in order to grasp this prize. Or, we could think about the rich young ruler, a nobleman collecting many fine things. He approaches Jesus looking to add righteousness to his assemblage of good things. He hungers for more, and that is not a bad thing. But Jesus finally challenges him with this: "If you wish to be perfect, go, sell your possessions, and give the money to the poor, and you will have treasure in heaven; then come, follow me" (Matt 19:21). Unlike the merchant seeking the costly pearl, *this* man was unwilling to lose it all to gain the prize. Matthew tells us, "he went away grieving, for he had many possessions" (19:22). The disciples turn to Jesus and ask him if true followers are doomed to be lowly and poor. Without hesitation, Jesus announces, "Truly, I tell you, at the renewal of all things, when the Son of Man is seated on the throne of his glory, you who have followed me will also sit on twelve thrones, judging the twelve tribes of Israel. And everyone who has left houses or brothers or sisters or father or mother or children or fields, for my name's sake, will receive a hundredfold, and will inherit eternal life" (19:16–29). This is the value of *Christian hope*, trusting by faith in the God who will eventually re-balance the scales of justice. And Paul makes a similar claim at the close of Phil 3: Believers live as members of a heavenly commonwealth and expect the visitation of the glorious rescuer, Lord Jesus Christ, who will turn their lowliness in resurrection glory and put all things right once and for all (3:20–21).

When I think about Paul's letter to the Philippians in general, and when we look at 3:7–21 in particular, I cannot help but be reminded of Tolkien's famous line: "all that is gold does not glitter." Paul, after all, is talking about the hidden value of knowing Christ, worth more than the merchant's costly pearl, but hidden in a field nevertheless. When I looked up Tolkien's whole poem a few months ago, I was stunned to see just how closely this matches Paul's message in Philippians (which is probably coincidental, I admit). Tolkien picks up on the themes of value (Phil 3:7–14), wandering/displacement (1:19), and light (2:15), but most appropriate to the end of Philippians 3 (vv. 20–21), Tolkien ends with royal eschatology, the renewal of all things through the emergence of the one and true king.

> All that is gold does not glitter,
> Not all those who wander are lost;

The old that is strong does not wither,
Deep roots are not reached by the frost.
From the ashes, a fire shall be woken,
A light from the shadows shall spring;
Renewed shall be blade that was broken,
The crownless again shall be king.
—Bilbo Baggins[4]

CONCLUSION

If Paul stepped away from more situational pragmatics (2:19–29) to talk more generally about Christian epistemology and valuing the cross of Christ in chapter 3, as we look ahead he touches back down again to *terra firma* to address a particular disagreement in the church between two women leaders. This opens up a broader discussion about dealing with worries and finding Christian joy and focusing on what is praiseworthy and beautiful.

DISCUSSION QUESTIONS

1. What would it mean for you to become a "friend of the cross"?

2. Re-read Tolkien's poem about "All that is gold does not glitter." What do you think he is trying to communicate? Which line(s) do you find most inspiring or interesting?

4. Tolkien, *Fellowship of the Ring,* 171.

6

KEEP CALM AND CARRY ON

Philippians 4:1–23

READING THE TEXT

A Call to Unity in the Gospel Mission (4:1–3)

1 So then, my dear brothers and sisters, my beloved and cherished, my joy and crown—stand strong in the Lord, beloved.

2 I urge Euodia and I urge Syntyche to think with one mind in the Lord. 3 Yes, and I also ask you, trustworthy yoke-fellow, assist these women, who have fought together in the gospel mission with me, along with Clement and the rest of my coworkers whose names appear in the Book of Life.

Keep Calm and Carry On (4:4–9)

4 Celebrate in the Lord always; I repeat, Celebrate! 5 Let all people know that you are gentle and generous. The Lord is near. 6 Don't be troubled. Instead let God know your requests which you make with a thankful heart, as you offer up prayers and petitions frequently. 7 Then peace from God, greater than any mind, will care after your hearts and thoughts in Christ Jesus. 8 Furthermore, my dear brothers and sisters:

Truth

Nobility

Justice

Perfection

Excellence

The Spectacular

Whatever showcases virtue and is worthy of respect—Let your mind dwell on such things. 9 Insomuch as you learned and receive and heard and saw such things from me, so you should do them as well. And the God of peace will be with you.

Sacrificial Partnership Renewed (4:10–20)

10 Now, I was so delighted in the Lord because finally you renewed your thoughtful care for me. (I know you were concerned before that, but did not get a chance to act until now.) 11 I am not saying this because I was physically desparate. In fact, I have learned how to be content no matter the situation. 12 I have experienced the lowest lows, and I have experienced the highest highs. In every situation and in all of life, God has taught me a secret—13 I always have

everything I need from the All-Powerful God, and this truth doesn't change whether I am full or hungry, rich or poor.[1]

14 Nevertheless, it was good of you to step in and carry some of the burden of my difficult situation. 15 I don't have to remind you, Philippians, that in the beginning of the gospel mission, when I left Macedonia, no church shared with me in a formal ministry partnership, which includes material support, except your community. 16 Even in Thessalonica, you sent aid a few times to meet my needs. 17 It is not the actual gift that matters to me; more important is the credit growing exponentially in your account. 18 I have received everything and I feel spoiled. I have more than enough from your gifts sent by Epaphroditus, they are a fragrant aroma, an acceptable sacrifice which pleases God. 19 And my God will satisfy any of your needs out of his massive wealth through Christ Jesus! 20 So let us honor God our Father for ever and ever, amen.

Final Greetings (4:21–23)

21 Greet every holy person in Christ Jesus. All the brothers and sisters with me send to you their well wishes. 22 All the holy people greet you, but especially those from Caesar's household. 23 May the grace of the Lord Jesus Christ be with each of your spirits.

---

1. Because 4:12–13 belong together as one idea, I blended some of the information together, so the versification is off a little bit from what you might see in a traditional English translation of these verses.

STUDYING THE TEXT

A Call to Unity in the Gospel Mission (4:1–3)

AT THE BEGINNING OF the fourth chapter of Philippians, Paul multiplies terms of endearment for this church: beloved (twice), brothers and sisters, cherished, "my joy and crown." This is not apostolic fluff or flattery. Paul regularly encourages his churches in his letters (e.g., 1 Thess 2:19), but this looks like a whole other level of intimacy and relationship. We get the sense that he had a unique friendship with this community. We learn from 4:10–20 that they chose to partner in his ministry at a level that no other church did. He calls them his "crown" probably because he sees in them the fullness of transformation by the gospel, such that they are models to other churches.

They were by no means perfect, though. Any church has areas of need and growth, and no church can settle in and become complacent. We get the sense that the Philippians were going through a number of challenges, so Paul repeats the essence of his exhortation from 1:27–30 in a more simplified form: "stand strong in the Lord" (4:1). This sounds a lot like military language, conjuring up images of an army facing a powerful enemy. They must steel themselves and be ready for battle.

One matter that Paul needed to address in this letter is the friction between two women in the church, Euodia and Syntyche. The mere fact of Paul mentioning these women in this letter implies that they had some prominence in the church. Theirs was not a personal spat, but something that clearly affected the whole church. Paul does not mention what roles they played in the church, but he does call them "coworkers" who have fought together in the gospel mission with him, and with other coworkers, their names are in the Book of Life. The mention of the Book of Life (4:3) strikes me as a way of acknowledging the valor and self-sacrificial leadership of these women, thus they certainly had some stature in the church. Perhaps they were church overseers or ministers (Phil 1:1). Whatever the case, they seem to have taken two different sides of an argument, and perhaps this divided the church as a whole (hence the call to a trusted "yoke-fellow" to intervene). One reasonable guess is that they were in conflict about whether or not to support Paul on an ongoing basis. Paul calls them to unity, not division. But the way he exhorts them is impressive. He does not call one to acquiesce to the other—he urges each one to equally step closer to the other for the sake of gospel unity in mission. To think with one mind is not to "cave," but to remember to put the mission above personal preferences and opinions. Paul is quick to commend *both* of them as ministry leaders; he does not "take sides." If the larger "battle" is to be won, God's people cannot be split and weakened. They must keep their eyes ahead, no watching their back for "friendly fire."

Keep Calm and Carry On (4:4–9)

Perhaps it is because we are comfortable with Bible-language that this doesn't seem strange to us, but it is genuinely odd, even bizarre, for a man in prison to urge others to "celebrate." But again in Philippians he repeats this order (twice; 4:4). Celebrate! Throw a party! Why? He doesn't come right out and say it, but God's people in Christ are meant to celebrate because the gospel is still spreading good news and power and joy and hope to people far and wide, and it still brings good things to the imprisoned (Paul) and the persecuted (the Philippians). Under the present circumstances, it appears that the Philippian Christians were troubled, anxious, and concerned. They were, what we would call, stressed out. Paul's counsel, especially in 4:5–9, is wise advice for *anyone* struggling with anxiety and discouragement due to stress.

First, he says something about their public character: "Let all people know that you are gentle and generous." Some older translations use the word "magnanimous." This is a disposition of care and concern for the *other*. Keep in mind, these Christians were being abused (verbally and socially, probably not physically), mocked, and scorned by unbelieving neighbors. It would cause anyone to be unnerved and on edge, frustrated and closed off. In the midst of this distress, Paul teaches (and models) generosity and grace towards any and everyone. Notice, he does not say: "be gentle"; he says, "let it be known about you by all that you are generous." That's a reputation, a pattern, a permanent disposition, a matter of one's innate and persistent character. This looks a lot like the advice he gives the Romans: "Do not repay anyone evil for evil, but take thought for what is noble in the sight of all" (Rom 12:17).

Paul abruptly follows this up with the statement, "the Lord is near." This could be Paul reminding them that the Lord is returning soon, but usually these types of statements are meant to challenge and warn his readers. Here, in a context where he wants to comfort them (and not stress them out more), that would be self-defeating. More likely, Paul means that the Philippian Christians can live out of their most generous self, because the Lord is close to them in presence, just as he writes a few verses later, "and the God of peace will be with you" (4:9).

Next Paul comforts and reassures the Philippian believers telling them not to be troubled. They should channel that nervous energy into praying. Normally, anxious hearts pray with fear and desperation, but Paul tells them to make requests to God with thanksgiving in their hearts (4:6). As

Jesus teaches, the Father knows what each person needs, even before they ask (Matt 6:8; see also 6:25–34). God does not always offer physical "solutions," like solving problems with a flick of a magic wand. Sometimes prayers are answered in such a way that the problem disappears, but often that is not how God operates. Later, Paul talks about his own experiences, and what God has offered is not always rescue or relief from a problem, but *contentment* and *perseverance*. Ultimately, what God promises that believers can rely on is God's own peace, greater than any mind, which ministers to heart and mind through Jesus Christ.

God's peace, though, doesn't simply get downloaded into human hearts. There are certain spiritual practices, commitments, and habits that welcome this peace. Paul lists out several values and virtues that should capture one's imagination in order to turn chaos into peace: truth, nobility, justice, perfect, and what is excellent and spectacular (4:8). The mind should choose to dwell on these things. This is another way of turning the anxious heart and mind to open itself up to all the goodness and light that is in the world. But he is quick to point out that this requires far more than pensive reflection on beauty in blissful repose. In 4:9 Paul refers to this excellence-oriented mentality as thought, action, and habit: "you should *do* them as well." This is Paul's formula for finding peace to overcome stress. This is not Paul's foolproof evidence, it is not comprehensive or universal; but it is wise counsel for developing virtues, habits, and practices to address anxiety.

Sacrificial Partnership Renewed (4:10–20)

The last major section of Philippians is a rather important one. In fact, it bookends the letter, as Paul first discussed his ministry partnership with them (1:6–7) so here he revisits their support for his gospel mission work. While virtually all scholars agree that in 4:10–20 Paul responds to their giving of aid to Paul through Epaphroditus, there is much debate about Paul's seeming hesitancy about *needing* their help. On the one hand, he expresses delight at their care for him (4:10, 14), their longterm support (4:15–16), and the overall satisfactory contribution they provided (4:18–19). On the other hand, he repeatedly refers to his ability to face hunger, poverty, and an austere lifestyle with contentment and trust in God (4:11–13, 17). For that reason, scholars have sometimes referred to this passage as Paul's "thankless thanks." He seems to be expressing appreciation for this gift from the Philippian church, but he also seems to go out of his way *not* to actually say "thank you." Some surmise it is because he doesn't want to seem like he is dependent on them and therefore would "owe" them (I am not convinced by that theory). Others believe it is because he treats them as "friends," and saying "thank you" would be too formal; friends don't need to say "thank you" (I don't buy that theory either). What I think is going on here is Paul expressing appreciation for the aid (4:10), but he ultimately points them in the direction of seeing how this offering is not *for Paul*, but a contribution to the wider gospel mission (4:17). He appreciates their sacrificial giving for the sake of what God is doing, not because they want to keep Paul alive. Paul knows that sooner or later he will die (2:17); he doesn't want to build churches in *his* honor. Rather, he wants to tie churches directly to God through Jesus Christ, so that, live or die, they contribute to the gospel mission.

In 4:10, he refers to their "renewed" giving and care—they had stopped giving, not because they found Paul suspicious, but perhaps due to a period of poverty. Paul takes a moment, though, to teach them about finding peace and contentment regardless of the circumstances. This is not just a theory or philosophy. Paul knew hard times; keep in mind, Roman prisons were not luxurious. He talks about God teaching him the secret of contentment. It is not really a complex method or mystery. It is quite simple: God takes care of his people no matter what. That doesn't mean food drops out of the sky. It *can* (and did with the manna feeding), but that is not always how God cares for his people. Sometimes the hungry stay hungry and the poor stay poor. Contentment is not about attaining to a certain level of comfort. It is about constantly feeding on the "bread" of the divine Word (Deut 8:3), relying on the presence and promise of God, because "the Lord is near" (see above Phil 4:5).

But Paul does not want to seem ungrateful (4:14). In fact, he is overjoyed by their ongoing support. Too many other churches failed to forge such a partnership (4:15–16). But he shows pride as their spiritual father insofar as they are growing in their faith and pleasing God with their obedience. If it comes at the expense of their financial comfort or security, Paul reminds them that God will take care of them too (4:19). This naturally leads Paul to praise the ever-present God who gives, and loves, and rewards his people.

Final Greetings (4:21–23)

Every Pauline letter contains final words, often with greetings from fellow believers. Paul sends his warm wishes and salutations to every saint or holy person in Jesus Christ. By singling out *every person*, Paul may be simply reminding them that everyone matters, from the doorkeeper to the overseer. Each one is holy and special, because each one belongs to Jesus Christ. Paul also sends to them greetings from the many brothers and sisters with him. I take this as Paul's expanding of their horizons. When we face problems, our world can become very small. We focus on our challenges and woes, and forget that there is a big, wide world out there. Paul may be reminding them that, even if they feel oppressed and anxious, God is doing glorious and marvelous things out there.

Paul sends special salutations from "those from Caesar's household." Keep in mind, this is not a reference to the imperial (blood) family. The Roman "household" referred to anyone that was associated with that estate, including hired workers (like the gardener and guard) as well as slaves—and the emperor had countless slaves in his service. Also, this imperial "household" was not restricted to Rome, but would include any outposts and estates associated with the emperor in strategic cities throughout the empire. Nevertheless, even if Paul were referring to imperial slaves who are Christians, he might have still meant this as an encouragement: the gospel is making inroads in Caesar's territory. Paul ends his letter to the Philippians with his classic wish of "grace." This is a message of love and care, trusting and hoping in the ongoing work of Jesus Christ to bless and lift up his holy people.

REFLECTING ON THE TEXT

The Hard Work of Reconciliation

The overarching exhortation of the final chapter of Philippians is: "stand strong in the Lord" (4:1). God's people are called to hard work for which temerity and fortitude are necessary. The first battle that Paul identifies in chapter 4 is for the sake of unity. This requires reconciliation where there is division. Paul does not offer a magic formula for helping those in disagreement to settle their differences. We will identify how he approaches the call to reconciliation, but it is less about following a specific protocol, and more about the attitude that each person has towards (a) the God of gospel and peace, (b) the other image-bearer, and (c) the self as servant of others.

We won't rehash the potential issues that caused problems between Euodia and Syntyche (see above). But Paul seems to approach the hope and hard work of reconciliation in this way.

The will to come together. Reconciliation begins with both sides desiring to come together.[2] Coming together is not about admitting fault. It is not about immediately forgiving and forgetting the wrong the other has done. It is simply a humble desire to be open to a path forward. The alternative is avoidance and rejection. Paul urges these women to come with open hearts and minds. It is subtle, but Paul wisely repeats the verb "I urge" so that he calls each person equally. He doesn't immediately presume which one should make the first step, he doesn't hint at which one is "more wrong." He turns to each person and warmly invites them to the table of conversation.

Starting with common ground. Paul's primary (and only stated) goal is that these women aim to "think with one mind in the Lord" (4:2). Some translations use the language of "agree," but this can come across as passive acquiescence. Paul does not urge one person to "give in" to the other. The language of thinking together *in the Lord* is about finding common ground, especially when it comes to ministry and mission. Often, when we are in conflict with other leaders, it is easy to see *only* differences. This can turn the other into the enemy. By beginning with a focus on *common mission*, hopefully the two parties can find common cause.

Use a facilitator. Paul calls upon a trustworthy ministry partner (perhaps Epaphroditus) to step in to "assist these women" (4:3). His role was not one of adjudicator, but of facilitator (or assistant). It is often helpful to have a third

2. See Volf, *Exclusion and Embrace.*

party who can bring an "objective" presence, not to decide on anything, but to be a calming presence.

Celebrate successes. Paul goes out of his way to commend both these women as coworkers in the gospel mission. His mention of their names being in the Book of Life (4:3) is probably a nod to their individual and equal contributions to ministry. Here Paul is inviting the church to celebrate both of their accomplishments. Surely it must make a difference in the work of reconciliation to start with celebration. What if a reconciliation session started with worship of God and celebration of the ministries of each person involved? This puts the matter in a wider perspective and points the whole process towards a bigger vision for the church.

Reconciliation is hard work. In the end, we don't actually know how things turned out for Euodia and Syntyche, and others involved in this disagreement. But we do know that if they resolved the matter, it would have taken commitment and grace. For Paul, Christian unity is a product of sustaining the mindset of Christ who did not grasp tightly to status or glory, but willingly humbled himself in view of the Father's will. There can be humility *and* truth, grace *and* justice. I would like to believe these women did just as Paul said, not because it was easy, but because they believed in the gospel mission—their lives were touched by the love of God—and they had support and help all along the way. Reconciliation is hard, but for Paul it is a symbol of and testimony to the saving work of God in Jesus Christ.

The Hard Work of Celebration Triumphing Over Worry

Life in the Roman world, two thousand years ago, is hard to imagine. No computers or phones. No microwaves or toasters. No cars or airplanes. No air conditioning or Tylenol.

No Google or GPS. Do we share *anything* in common with people set apart by such a great amount of time? Yes: *stress*. To be human is to experience anxiety. The cause of the anxiety might change from one person to the next, or in a different era or context, but mortals have always had troubling troubles. The ancient Greek writer Hippocrates of Cos recounts two phobia cases (see *Epidemic* 5.81). A certain Nicanor would go to a dinner party, but at the sound of flutes would experience "masses of terrors." The problem was not flute music per se—he was fine if he heard flutes during the day. It was specifically as a trigger related to the parties, perhaps some kind of social anxiety. Another man, Democles, had a terrible fear of heights and falling (5.82). Stoic philosopher Cicero distinguished between mental affliction (*molestia*), worry (*sollicitudo*), and anxiety (*angor*), and recognized that problems in the human life of the mind could lead to bodily problems (*Tusc. Disp.* 3.10). Many of us can identify. (I went to the ER for an anxiety attack last year—I thought I was having a heart attack.) We can certainly also resonate with Jesus's teaching from the Sermon on the Mount:

> Therefore I tell you, do not worry about your life, what you will eat or what you will drink, or about your body, what you will wear. Is not life more than food, and the body more than clothing? Look at the birds of the air; they neither sow nor reap nor gather into barns, and yet your heavenly Father feeds them. Are you not of more value than they? And can any of you by worrying add a single hour to your span of life? And why do you worry about clothing?
>
> Consider the lilies of the field, how they grow; they neither toil nor spin, yet I tell you, even Solomon in all his glory was not clothed like one of these. But if God so clothes the grass

of the field, which is alive today and tomorrow is thrown into the oven, will he not much more clothe you—you of little faith? Therefore do not worry, saying, "What will we eat?" or "What will we drink?" or "What will we wear?" For it is the Gentiles who strive for all these things; and indeed your heavenly Father knows that you need all these things. But strive first for the kingdom of God and his righteousness, and all these things will be given to you as well. So do not worry about tomorrow, for tomorrow will bring worries of its own. Today's trouble is enough for today. (Matt 6:25–34)

We don't know exactly what was troubling the Philippians (Lack of money? Food? Clothing? Problems with work? Relationships? Religious issues?). But we can make an educated guess that it was combination of social persecution from outsiders, friction within the church, concern for Epaphroditus, and uncertainty about Paul. And we can infer that such stress factors were leading some to become agitated (see Phil 2:14). *What do you do when you are bogged down with stress? When all seems dark and impossible?*

Before reflecting theologically on Paul's advice here, let me say that he and Jesus both were addressing what we might call common or basic worries, not mental disorders. In some circumstances, it is wise to seek a medical professional; Paul's counsel is general and theological, not clinical. Having said that, many of us (including myself) need help managing stress and anxiety, and Paul offers much wisdom.

Celebrate! If I were a Philippian Christian, I might become irritated at this point in the letter that Paul continues to offer the remedy of "celebration." Sometimes you don't want or need to celebrate. Smiles and glee are not a cure-all. But we have to keep in mind that Paul was not just calling for meaningless jubilance. Rather, it is celebrating *in the*

Lord, and *because of the Lord*. True Christian joy recognizes the miraculous and grace-filled presence of God. How often Christians fail to recognize their blessings right in front of them, Paul would say. Consider a similar message in Hebrews. The writer observes how the great patriarchs heard the promises of God of redemption and fulfillment and "greeted them" from a distance (11:13). While they fought for the faith and trusted and hoped in God, they died before these promises were realized (11:39–40). Alternatively, those who know Jesus and are filled with the Holy Spirit are part of an indestructible kingdom (12:28), and so we ought to be thankful for what we are blessed with (12:28–29). So Paul calls twice for celebration.

Look outward. Worry is often all-consuming. Stress and anxiety can have the affect of turning us inward with an overly protective spirit. We can become selfish as a defense mechanism to stress. Paul frustrates this process by calling Christians to live magnanimously, gaining a reputation for being both gentle and generous. But how can weak mortals fight the insulating mechanism caused by stress and turn outward? Paul's short and simple answer is "The Lord is near." I didn't really understand what this meant until I inherited a prayer course from my colleague MaryKate Morse. I gladly used the textbook that she wrote called *A Guidebook to Prayer*.[3] Each week we would try one of the prayer practices she describes in her book. One of the exercises most impactful for me was called "Rest Prayer." I used to assume prayer was about talking and telling God things. But Rest Prayer resists talking or doing anything. It is simply resting in God. Resting as a form of prayer "draws the heart and body back to God's overaching love and sovereign will. Rest calibrates us and brings us back to the center. Rest is a trust response to God's love. Rest reminds

3. Morse, *A Guidebook to Prayer.*

us that ultimately our significance is in our love relationship with God and not in our productivity."[4] When Christians actively trust and rest in the God who is near, they are in a better position to face fears and potential problems. Indeed, Paul encourages prayer to God, but not anxious prayer. Rather, believers can even pray with a thankful heart (Phil 4:6). This is not delusional, but hope-filled, because Christians trust the God who has already brought the good news into the world.

Use your imagination. In 4:8, Paul places in front of the troubled Philippians a list of values and virtues for their meditation and practice. It is not an exhaustive list, but representative of all that is good and beautiful and right in the world. We need constant reminders that signs of God's creative beauty are all around us if we just look. The items he lists are not specifically *Christian* virtues; these items would be prized and appreciated by moralists throughout the Roman empire. Paul can feel comfortable naming and prizing these things because all humans were created by God to love beauty, pursue justice, aspire to excellence, and wonder at the spectacular. Part of what it means to be made in the image of God is to pursue greatness. This doesn't make humans prideful. It means that as guardians and stewards of creation, we were designed to reflect God's glory in the world using our own creative capacities to design, support, and nurture great things. When we experience limitations, stress, and anxiety, this serves as a healthy reminder that there is so much beauty and goodness in the world beyond our present sorrows.

As part of my job, I work closely with pastors in ministry. You may know that pastors experience quite a lot of stress as they serve their communities throughout the week, advocating for the needy, comforting the bereaved,

4. Morse, *A Guidebook to Prayer*, 52.

and walking with the sick.[5] An element of my role is to help pastors find balance, peace, and resilience in the midst of their hectic lives. One of my recommendations, based in part on Phil 4:8, is to have daily rituals of beauty and excellence.[6] What I recommend is for people with stressful situations or jobs to build in small, but regular times of meditation on or interaction with something wonderful; to admire it, reflect on it, enjoy it. For me, for example, it involves taking 5 minutes in the morning to make a fresh homemade latte (with cinnamon, honey, and cardamom!). The sounds, smells, and careful crafting are part of my routine and I look forward to it every single morning. For some, it might be spending a few minutes listening to excellent classical music—Yo-Yo Ma on the cello is my personal favorite. For others, it might be surrounding yourself with art in your office, and just taking a bit of time at the end of the day to soak it in.

For me, personally, I used to feel guilty indulging in these sorts of things, imagining they were frivolous, a waste of time. But what changed is my awareness of my own health. Yes, my physical health, but also my emotional health as well. Life is full of difficult things, and part of managing and overcoming them is to feed and strengthen our imagination. Busy, stressed-out people should not make the excuse that they have "no time" for beauty or the spectacular. They need it more than anyone else. Part of this, then, is simply trusting God, that he knows us better than we know ourselves. If you are dealing with anxiety right now, or suffer

5. View the Lifeway Research report from 2015: https://lifewayresearch.com/pastorprotection/.

6. I have also benefited from the incredibly rich research and insight from Matthew Bloom and his work on "Flourishing in Ministry": http://www.bomlibrary.org/wp-content/uploads/2018/03/FiM-2018.pdf.

from chronic stress factors on your life, I encourage you to stop right now and think about how you can build rituals of excellence and beauty into your life.

The Hard Work of the Contented Life

Contentment does not mean endless glee. And it doesn't mean "no problems." That would be the perfect life, and Paul never presents that as an option. Contentment is sometimes defined as "quiet satisfaction." It is the soul anchored by peace. Some problems we face are beyond our control. Other problems we invite on ourselves because we experience a restless anxiousness for more success or power, or we are afraid of being small or insignificant. Paul was not above dealing with stress (see 1 Thess 3:5), but in Philippians he explains that God taught him a secret (4:12). It is not some magic formula or mantra for happiness; rather, it is the secret of trusting that God knows what he is doing and he cares for his children (4:13). That doesn't mean that hard times don't happen. Paul had plenty of them. But he also had thrilling, rejuvenating, and joy-filled moments. Life is naturally full of ups and downs. The trick is to figure how to ride this roller coaster of life for the long run.

The ancient Jewish sage Ben Sira talks about a man's ability to find contentment, rich or poor, as long as he has a good wife and a good reputation (Sir 26:4). He also teaches that mortals need only water, bread, clothing, and a simple home (29:21). Too many people, he explains, get caught up in seeking to get invited to fancy parties and pursuing the lifestyle of the rich and famous. Good guests are not there for the food, but for the friendship (29:23–24). Beware, or else others will start to use *you* for your amenities (29:25–26).

When Paul writes about contentment, he is often referring to the repulsion of two vices: greed and glory. As for the latter, Paul had to learn the hard way that Christ-followers will live with shame in this world. So, Paul was taught how to focus his identity *not* on the opinions of the masses, but on God alone: "Therefore I am content with weaknesses, insults, hardships, persecutions, and calamities for the sake of Christ; for whenever I am weak, then I am strong" (2 Cor 12:10).

The second obstacle to finding contentment for Paul is greed. Again, this is something that translates into every generation and culture. In 1 Timothy, Paul observes those who seek the status and security of wealth. Rather than bringing fulfillment, Paul claims that such aspirations lead to ruin (1 Tim 6:9; cf. Heb 13:5–6). Rather than bringing ease and luxury, it causes pain and infects the heart (6:10). Hoarding riches is meaningless, because we "brought nothing into the world, so that we can take nothing out of it" (6:7). Like Ben Sira, Paul urges his readers to be satisfied with the simple life of basic food[7] and clothing.

One of the keys to finding this elusive contentment for Paul is this: ignoring the *noise*. Society is always very busy and we always want to be advertising our successes, and looking around to see who is *more* successful than us. Today, with social media, we have never-ending access to this kind of noise, everyone constantly sharing about all the fun

---

7. I would like to make the important point that basic food does not necessarily always mean the cheapest food. The reality is that big corporation grocery stores sometimes underpay farmers and suppliers and cut corners to deliver on "low prices." I believe Paul would not encourage Christians today to seek the bargain price at the cost of shackling farm workers and food producers to poverty; the evidence is well documented; see http://fortune.com/longform/cheap-groceries-food-farmers-laborers/; and https://bcorporation.net/about-b-corps.

and exciting things they are doing. (*How is everyone always in Hawaii?*) And we are tempted to either broadcast our own happiness, or lurk with envy and resentment. I know, for me, I have had to unfollow some full-time vacationers. In view of this noise that surrounds us, Paul writes to the Thessalonians, "make it your ambition to lead a quiet life" (1 Thess 4:11 NIV). The way Paul words this command, it includes a twist of irony. First, he uses the language of ambition and striving (*philotimeomai*): *pursue, chase, hunt*. This is what we do when we pour all of our energy toward one goal or objective. We would expect something grand to follow after this kind of verb. But Paul writes that what should be hotly pursued is "quiet" or "stillness" (*esuchazō*). What does this mean? In the same verse he refers to focusing on your own affairs and working with your own hands. For Paul, the quiet or peaceful life is not chilling out in the woods meditating somewhere (not that there is anything wrong with that on occasion). It is about a simple life filled with good, honest labor, and enjoying the world, work, family, and friends without getting caught up in all the noise of wondering "whose life is better."

Even according to Paul's own experience, I cannot stress enough how important friendships are to living peaceful and happy lives. The "quiet life" is not a life cut off from others. Paul goes out of his way to express his jubilance at the Philippians' renewal of their support for him (Phil 4:10) and how special it is that they have invested in his ministry from the beginning (Phil 1:6; 4:15). He refers to them as his beloved friends and "cherished" companions (4:1). Paul could be contented, even in prison, knowing both that God would look after him, but also that he had friends who cared for him as well. Part of the reason I have referred to "contentment" as "hard work" is because it requires developing interdependent relationships where each one in the community is looked after (2 Cor 8:14–15). Yes, peace is a state of mind, but deep and lasting peace requires a community where life is shared with its inevitable ups and downs.

We see glimpses of this shared life in the final greetings of Philippians. No matter what difficulties the Philippian believers were facing, they had the grace of the Lord Jesus Christ and the support and prayers of God's people around the world (Phil 4:22–23). For Paul, even in chains, that was enough to find peace and joy in his spirit.

DISCUSSION QUESTIONS

1. When you have sought to reconcile with someone, what techniques have worked and not worked?

2. How do you handle anxiety and stress in your life? What kind of habits and support systems would help you maintain peace and contentment?

7

WHAT ARE SCHOLARS SAYING ABOUT PHILIPPIANS?

THROUGHOUT THE MAJORITY OF this book, we have offered an introduction of the basic issues involved in reading Philippians with minimal direct reference to academic scholarship. While the exposition has been based on the state of academic study of Philippians, we have limited interaction with particular scholars and theories. Some readers of this book, though, are undoubtedly eager to get a sense for currents in Philippians scholarship. Here we will offer a set of soundings in key contributions to the study of Philippians from the last twenty years. In order to organize this scholarship in a sensible way, we will use the basic categories of "The World Behind the Text" (background, context, situation), "The World of the Text" (the letter to the Philippians itself), and "The World in Front of the Text" (the reception, interpretation, and application of Philippians).

THE WORLD BEHIND THE TEXT

Of any of the categories we will discuss in this chapter, this seems to be where most of the academic energy lies. That is probably because we are learning more and more about the Roman Empire from archaeology, as well as new insights into the sociological, religious, and politics dynamics of that world. This has raised major questions about how early Christians interacted within and negotiated their world.

In the late 1990s and early 2000s, Richard Ascough took an interest in Greco-Roman voluntary associations and how these might help us to understand better Christ groups such as we see in Philippi. These associations were groups of men and/or women who came together regularly based on some commonality. There were different types of associations, professional ones for laborers of the same skills, burial clubs to ensure a proper funeral, and religious associations. Ascough argues that the Philippian church would have resembled a "religious association" to outsiders. Such connections, Ascough argues, could explain things like structure, leadership, and gender roles within the church, even if the believers did not consciously or intentionally identify themselves as a religious association.[1] Another important study of the ancient context of Philippians is by Peter Oakes. In his book, *Philippians: From People to Letter,* Oakes sets out to reconstruct the social and economic identities of the letter's first recipients.[2] He

1. See Ascough, *Paul's Macedonian Associations;* see also Ascough, "What Are They *Now,*" 207–44.

2. Oakes, *Philippians: From People to Letter;* for a brief summary by the author see Oakes, "Philippians: From People to Letter," 371–74.

also fleshes out what suffering and persecution would have looked like in that environment. Along the way, he debunks several myths that are popularly repeated; for example, Oakes argues that most of the Philippian Christians would have been Greeks, and very few would have been Roman citizens. In 2005, Joseph Hellerman wrote a fascinating study called *Reconstructing Honor in Roman Philippi.*[3] His goal was to demonstrate how "Roman" the city of Philippi was in culture and values, especially based on inscriptional evidence. Along these lines, he cogently demonstrates how honor- and status-oriented these people were in general. This affects how one reads Paul's letter, especially the subversive nature of Christ's humility in the so-called Christ Hymn (Phil 2:5–11). In my opinion, Hellerman's work is the most important historical research on Philippians in the last quarter of a century.

Several recent works have attempted to examine how the Philippian Christians related to both Jews and gentiles in society. Much of this work takes interest in who persecuted the Philippian believers, why, and what the church's reaction was. In the past, scholars often presumed persecution against the Philippians was predominantly by Jewish groups, but more and more there is a recognition that the persecution probably had political elements and, thus, came from civic authorities or groups loyal to Roman political interests.[4]

There is also ongoing work on the specific situation that gave rise to Paul's letter to the Philippians. One reason Paul wrote this letter pertains to his ministry partnership

3. Hellerman, *Reconstructing Honor*; see also his helpful commentary, *Philippians.*

4. See Tellbe, *Paul between Synagogue and State.* For a recent study that dwells extensively on method in detecting and identifying opponents, see Nikki, *Opponents and Identity.*

with the Philippians. Mark Jennings argues—persuasively in my view—that Paul had a strategic concern to maintain a strong relationship of mutual support with the Philippians.[5] In terms of Paul's situation, Craig S. Wansink sheds light on what Roman imprisonment would have been like for the apostle.[6] Of course, there is ongoing debate about *where* (and *when*) Paul was in prison when he wrote Philippians.[7] In more recent years, biblical scholars have put their heads together with classicists and historians to view Paul as a kind of moral philosopher. Phil 4:8 continues to be an intriguing text where Paul lists out several values and virtues that resemble very closely ideas of Roman morality and excellence as well.

THE WORLD OF THE TEXT

We will not take time here to talk about the scholarship on individuals passages in Philippians (except the Christ Hymn, see below). But Andy Johnson has recently written a helpful digest of the best commentaries on Philippians (as well as Colossians, Philemon, 1–2 Thessalonians, and the Pastoral Epistles).[8] On the Christ Hymn (2:5–11), continual study of this fascinating text has carried on unabated. Gregory Fewster wrote a useful summary of scholarship in 2015.[9] Matthew Gordley has freshly reexamined the Philippian Christ Hymn by comparing it to hymns and psalmody

---

5. See Jennings, *Price of Partnership*.

6. See Wansink, *Chained in Christ*.

7. For a brief discussion of the state of scholarship on this, see Hansen, *Letter to the Philippians*, 20–24.

8. See https://www.catalystresources.org/building-a-new-testament -library-philippians-philemon-6/.

9. Fewster, "Philippians Christ Hymn," 191–206.

produced by Jews, Greeks, and Romans in antiquity.[10] Such poetic works, he argues, often have essential teaching functions for a community. The elevation of Jesus in the Christ Hymn is not simply a religious notion, but would have had political significance as well—Jesus as name confessed and before whom all bow means that he is greater than the emperor, a dangerous song indeed. Along these lines, community songs could play an important role as resistance poetry, with many precedents in the Old Testament. Daniel Fabricatore wrote an extensive study of the language of "form" in Phil 2:6–7.[11] While it was once widely assumed that the *morphē* of Christ pertained to his "nature," Fabricatore argues that it is more accurate to follow the more common use of *morphē* as "outward appearance." This does not imply that Christ was only divine in *appearance*; it points to his visible splendor that he had to relinquish to take the *morphē* of a slave out of humility, and out of obedience to the Father.

Another industrious conversation on Philippians relates to the letter's genre or type. Professional letter-writers in antiquity often followed conventional epistolary forms. In the 1990s, a group of scholars took interest in what seemed to be "friendship" language in Philippians. This led to a classification of the epistle as a "letter of friendship."[12] For several years, this classification became quite popular, but is now receiving significant pushback. Many have pointed out that, while certainly Paul is "friendly" in this letter, he seems to go out of his way to avoid formal language of friendship (*philia, philos*).[13] Loveday Alexander

10. Gordley, *New Testament Christological Hymns*.

11. Fabricatore, *Form of God*.

12. See Stowers, "Friends and Enemies," 105–21.

13. Still has written an excellent critique: "More than Friends?," 64–66.

posits that it would better be identified as a "family letter," where the goal would be to reinforce the bonds of affection of a household.[14] Paul Holloway prefers to read Philippians as a "letter of consolation," which served the purpose of turning grief and discouragement into joy and relief. He offers many parallels from Greco-Roman texts as well as Jewish ones.[15] The genre and form questions are important, because it signals rhetorical intent and helps to elucidate the situation behind the text and the purpose of the text. Unfortunately, these conversations can suffer from circular reasoning, and at the moment many have simply concluded that either Philippians does not fit *any* standard letter type, or it is some kind of mixed type.

THE WORLD IN FRONT OF THE TEXT

Interpreters are also becoming more and more aware of how we read and "receive" the ancient text of Philippians, throughout history and today as well. Thinking about the interpretation of Philippians throughout the years, there are a couple of handy resources. First, we can mention the Ancient Christian Commentary on Scripture, volume 8, which compiles perspectives and quotes from the church fathers on Galatians, Ephesians, and Philippians.[16] More recently, InterVarsity Press has invested in the Reformation Commentary on Scripture; check out Graham Tomlin's volume on Philippians and Colossians.[17]

---

14. Alexander, "Hellenistic Letter-Forms," 87–101.

15. See Holloway, *Consolation in Philippians*; his new commentary fills this approach out with more exegetical discussion; see *Philippians*.

16. Edwards, *Galatians, Ephesians, Philippians*.

17. Tomlin, *Philippians and Colossians*.

When it comes to examinations of the theology of Philippians, as one might expect, there are vigorous ongoing conversations about the Christology of Philippians, especially in relation to the Christ Hymn (see above).[18] But there has developed interest as well in the Christology demonstrated in Phil 3:7–11.[19] Questions and discussions revolve around what it means to "know Christ," to enter into his suffering and death, and experience his resurrection.

Perhaps the theological discussion that has received the most attention in recent years is about mission and evangelism in Philippians. In 2008, Brian Peterson made the case that Paul's letter to the Philippians shows no signs that he encouraged that church to vocally evangelize their unbelieving neighbors. Rather, their living out of the gospel was about worshiping God and representing the work of New Creation in the world.[20] They were meant to be a community *displaying* the gospel, not *delivering* it. But James P. Ware has argued the opposite. Ware posits that Paul, inspired by a prophetic vision for the conversion of the nations, would have expected his converts to share the good news with everyone.[21] In part, this conversation relates to whether the Greek verb in 2:16 (*epechō*) should be translated as "holding fast to the word of life" (which might imply worship, lifestyle, obedience) or "holding forth the word of life" (which might imply engaging in mission and evangelism in verbal proclamation of the gospel). Michael Gorman and Dean Flemming have called for a both/and that attempts to transcend this dichotomy.[22]

18. See Tilling, *Paul's Divine Christology*; Capes, *Divine Christ*.

19. Koperski, *Knowledge of Christ Jesus*. See also Byrnes, *Conformation*.

20. See Peterson, "Being the Church," 163–78.

21. See Ware, *Paul and the Mission*.

22. Gorman, *Becoming the Gospel*; see also Flemming, *Recovering*.

In terms of how to reflect on the theological messages of Philippians for today, there are several great resources in modern scholarship. The book *Dwelling with Philippians* is a wonderfully creative, dynamic engagement with Philippians.[23] The editors present this book as an "unhurried contemplative response to the mystery, beauty and life-changing power of the text."[24] It is full of inspiring images related to the text, poems and hymns, and spiritual reflections. A more classic treatment of the theology of Philippians can be found in I. Howard Marshall's portion of the book *The Theology of the Shorter Pauline Letters*.[25] Unsurprisingly, Marshall gives special attention to the themes of humility and unity in Philippians. In more recent theological work on Philippians, Lynn Cohick underscores love and grace in the midst of suffering, and Stephen Fowl gives special attention to the topic of friendship in theological perspective.[26]

SUMMARY AND CONCLUSION

Over the years, Philippians has maintained its place as one of the most fascinating books of the Bible, and an energetic place for academic discussion. For ages the concentration remained on theoretic and theological questions pertaining to the godhead, especially the nature and divinity of Christ. But we have seen a growing fascination with the world around and of the Philippian church. In the middle of the twentieth century, the focus was largely on this church's relationship to (and especially conflict with) Jews and Judaism. In more recent years, it has expanded to the Roman

---

23. Steele Halstead et al., *Dwelling with Philippians*.
24. Steele Halstead et al., *Dwelling with Philippians*, ix.
25. Donfried and Marshall, *Shorter Pauline Letters*.
26. Cohick, *Philippians*; Fowl, *Philippians*.

world at large and social relationships on various levels (gender, economics, politics, etc.). At the same time, there are robust theological conversations on the nature and mission of the church.

DISCUSSION QUESTIONS

1. What lingering questions do you have about the background and situation of the text, or the meaning of particular passages?

2. I encourage you to read Philippians in 3 different translations. What differences between them do you notice?

BIBLIOGRAPHY

Alexander, Loveday. "Hellenistic Letter-Forms and the Structure of Philippians." *JSNT* 37 (1989) 87–101.

Ascough, Richard S. *Paul's Macedonian Associations: The Social Context of Philippians and 1 Thessalonains.* WUNT 2.161. Tübingen: Mohr Siebeck, 2003.

———. "What Are They *Now* Saying about Christ Groups and Associations?" *CBR* 13 (2015) 207–44.

Bakirtzis, Charalambos, and Helmut Koester, ed. *Philippi at the Time of Paul and After His Death.* Harrisburg, PA: Trinity International Press, 1998.

Beker, J. C. *Paul the Apostle.* Philadelphia: Fortress, 1980.

Bonhoeffer, Dietrich. *Letters and Papers from Prison.* Minneapolis: Fortress Press, 2010.

Boring, M. Eugene. *An Introduction to the New Testament.* Louisville, KY: Westminster John Knox, 2012.

Byrnes, Michael. *Conformation to the Death of Christ and the Hope of Resurrection.* Rome: Pontificia Università Gregoriana, 2003.

Capes, David B. *The Divine Christ.* Grand Rapids: Baker, 2018.

Cohick, Lynn. *Philippians.* SOGBC. Grand Rapids: Zondervan, 2013.

Dodd, Brian J. *The Problem with Paul.* Downers Grove, IL: InterVarsity, 1996.

Donfried, Karl and I. Howard Marshall. *The Theology of the Shorter Pauline Letters.* NTT. Cambridge: Cambridge University Press, 1993.

Edwards, Mark J., ed. *Galatians, Ephesians, Philippians.* ACCS. Downers Grove, IL: IVP, 1999.

Fabricatore, Daniel. *Form of God, Form of A Servant : An Examination of the Greek Noun "Morphe" in Philippians 2:6-7.* Lanham, MD; Plymouth: University Press of America, 2010.

Fewster, Gregory. "The Philippians Christ Hymn: Trends in Critical Scholarship." *CBR* 13 (2015) 191–206.

Flemming, Dean. *Recovering the Full Mission of God: A Biblical Perspective on Being, Doing, and Telling.* Downers Grove, IL: InterVarsity, 2013.

Fowl, Stephen. *Philippians.* THNT. Grand Rapids: Eerdmans, 2005.

Garland, David. *1 Corinthians.* BECNT. Grand Rapids: Baker, 2003.

Gordley, Matthew. *New Testament Christological Hymns.* Downers Grove, IL: InterVarsity, 2018.

Gorman, Michael J. *Becoming the Gospel.* Grand Rapids: Eerdmans, 2015.

———. *Elements of Biblical Exegesis.* Grand Rapids: Baker, 2009.

Hansen, G. Walter. *The Letter to the Philippians.* PNTC. Grand Rapids: Eerdmans, 2009.

Hellerman, Joseph. *Embracing Shared Ministry.* Grand Rapids: Kregel, 2013.

———. "The Humiliation of Christ in the Social World of Roman Philippi." *BibSac* 160 (2003) 321–36.

———. *Philippians.* EGGNT. Nashville: Broadman & Holman, 2015.

———. *Reconstructing Honor in Roman Philippi: Carmen Christi as Cursus Pudorum.* SNTSMS. Cambridge: Cambridge University Press, 2005.

Holloway, Paul A. *Consolation in Philippians: Philosophical Sources and Rhetorical Strategy.* SNTSMS. Cambridge: Cambridge University Press, 2001.

———. *Philippians.* Hermeneia. Minneapolis: Fortress, 2017.

Hooker, M. D. "Philippians." NIB 11. Nashville: Abingdon, 1996.

Jennings, Mark. *The Price of Partnership in the Letter of Paul to the Philippians.* LNTS 578. London: T. & T. Clark, 2017.

Koperski, Veronica. *The Knowledge of Christ Jesus My Lord.* Kampen: Kok Pharos, 1996.

Morse, MaryKate. *A Guidebook to Prayer.* Downers Grove, IL: InterVarsity, 2013.

Nikki, Nina. *Opponents and Identity in Philippians.* Supplements to Novum Testamentum 173. Boston: Brill, 2018.

Oakes, Peter. *Philippians: From People to Letter.* SNTSMS. Cambridge: Cambridge University Press, 2000.

———. "Philippians: From People to Letter." *TyndBul* 47 (1996) 371–74.

Peterson, Brian. "Being the Church in Philippi." *HBT* 30 (2008) 163–78.

Richards, E. R. *First-Century Letter Writing*. Downers Grove, IL: InterVarsity, 2004.

Seneca. *On Listening*. In *Seneca, Epistles, Volume IV*. Loeb Classical Library 75. Cambridge: Harvard University Press, 1917.

Steele Halstead, Elizabeth, et al. *Dwelling with Philippians*. Grand Rapids: Eerdmans, 2010.

Still, Todd D. "More than Friends? The Literary Classification of Philippians Revisited." *PRS* 39 (2012) 64–66.

Stowers, Stanley K. "Friends and Enemies in the Politics of Heaven: Reading Theology in Philippians." In *Pauline Theology: Thessalonians, Philippians, Galatians, Philemon*, edited by J. M. Bassler, 105–21. Minneapolis: Fortress, 1991.

Tellbe, Mikael. *Paul between Synagogue and State: Christians, Jews and Civic Authorities in 1 Thessalonians, Romans and Philippians*. ConBNT 34. Stockholm: Almqvist & Wiksell, 2001.

Tilling, Chris. *Paul's Divine Christology*. Grand Rapids: Eerdmans, 2015.

Tolkien, J. R. R. *The Fellowship of the Ring*. 2nd ed. Boston: Houghton Mifflin, 2001.

Tomlin, Graham. *Philippians and Colossians*. Reformation Commentary on Scripture 11. Downers Grove, IL: InterVarsity, 2013.

Volf, Miroslav. *Exclusion and Embrace*. Nashville: Abingdon, 2010.

Wansink, Craig. *Chained in Christ: The Experience and Rhetoric of Paul's Imprisonments*. JSNTSup 130. Sheffield: Sheffield Academic, 1996.

Ware, James P. *Paul and the Mission of the Church*. Grand Rapids: Baker, 2011.

Watson, David. *Honor Among Christians*. Minneapolis: Fortress, 2011.

Winter, Bruce. *Divine Honours for the Caesars*. Grand Rapids: Eerdmans, 2015.

Wright, N. T. *Paul: A Biography*. New York: HarperOne, 2018.

NAMES INDEX

Names Index

ANCIENT DOCUMENT INDEX